GW00455860

FOR YOU THE WAR IS OVER

FOR YOU THE WAR IS OVER

The Hon. Philip Kindersley

MIDAS BOOKS

First published UK in 1983 by
MIDAS BOOKS
12 Dene Way, Speldhurst
Tunbridge Wells, Kent TN3 0NX

Copyright © The Hon. Philip Kindersley 1983

ISBN 0 85936 114 4 (UK)

First published USA in 1983 by
HIPPOCRENE BOOKS INC.
171 Madison Avenue
New York, NY 10016

ISBN 0-88254-744-5 (USA)

All rights reserved. No part of this publication may be
reproduced, stored in a retrieval system, or transmitted
in any form or by any means, electronic, mechanical,
photocopying or otherwise, without the prior permission
of Midas Books.

Printed and bound in Great Britain by
Billings Ltd., Worcester.

TO THOSE KIND PEOPLE WHOSE LETTERS
DID SO MUCH TO CHEER UP THE WEARY
DAYS OF CAPTIVITY.

Contents

Preface

This was my third attempt to write this story. The first effort began at Campo Concentramento No. 49 at Fontanellato, a British officers' prisoner of war camp in northern Italy. A hasty exit to avoid the Germans in September 1943 necessitated the manuscript being left behind.

I then lived for seven weeks in the Apennines, near the small town of Bardi in the province of Parma. During this period I started the story again, writing it in notebooks supplied by the local school-teacher. After completing some four hundred pages, I started the trek south towards the British lines. Between Gubbio and Perugia I was chased and captured by Fascist militia, and during the hunt was forced to throw away my notebooks, which also contained letters from friendly Italians whom I had no wish to compromise.

My next destination was a German prison camp, Oflag VIIIF, at Märisch Trubau in Czechoslovakia. There were no notebooks available, so the story was written on cardboard from old Canadian biscuit boxes. Had this version gone astray, I would have accepted that the story was never meant to be printed.

PLK

1
Tunis

When dawn broke on Christmas morning 1942, I was sitting in a slit trench on a hill some twenty-odd miles from the city of Tunis. A German attack was expected at any moment. We did not have to wait long, as shortly after we had wished each other a Merry Christmas the Germans sent their seasonal greetings in the form of whistling mortar bombs. I am not going to describe the ensuing battle. Many good fellows spent their last Christmas on that hill. I was taken prisoner by the Germans.

What strange things one thinks of in the middle of battle! While the mortar bombs were falling all around us, I kept looking at my watch and wondering what the people at home were doing. I pictured them first going off to early service then gathering at the breakfast table, where the exchange of presents would be taking place. I pictured the mass of tissue paper and coloured ribbon – the most important part of a Christmas parcel – which would be littering the table. I imagined the excited cries of the children as they opened their parcels. It all seemed so far away – and there we were trying to kill each other on that Christmas morning. It all seemed so utterly futile.

My company position was finally surrounded, and the survivors were taken prisoner. I was the only officer left, but the Germans would not allow me to stay with the men. I was accordingly sent off to the German battle HQ with a young German soldier as my escort. We walked along in silence until he offered me a cigarette; then, finding that I could speak a little German, my companion expressed his disgust at having to fight on Christmas Day.

While walking along, I saw the bodies of five men from my battalion lying about fifteen feet to the right of the road. I asked my escort if I could walk over and identify them; the German agreed, and we both walked over to where the men were lying. The mere fact that the bodies were so close together should have put me on my guard, but as I had had no sleep for twenty-four hours my brain was not working very quickly.

I had just identified one of the bodies as that of a sergeant in the battalion when some other Germans further up the road shouted out: 'Mines! Mines!' My escort motioned me to move away, but we had not walked more than a few paces before there was a terrific explosion, and I felt myself lifted in the air. The next thing I knew, I was on my back in the road feeling as if I had a hundred holes through me. I looked round for my German escort and saw the poor fellow lying a few feet away from me. He had been blown to bits from the waist down; death must have been instantaneous. He had trodden on the mine and taken the full force of the explosion between his legs, thereby saving me from serious injury. I had had a miraculous escape, as I was only three feet away from him at the time of the explosion.

I continued to sit on the road in a dazed condition, wondering how badly I had been hit. I felt pain in my right leg, right arm and in the centre of my back. My left wrist was bleeding, and I felt the blood running down the back of my neck from a wound in my head.

In the meantime, the other Germans had come back to help us. One of them, although he must have been a good thirty yards away at the time, had a bad wound in his hand from one of the mine splinters. After looking at their dead comrade, they turned their attention to me, whereupon I was violently sick, and fainted.

When I came round again, two or three Germans were standing over me. They seemed very excited and immediately started to tell me what a lucky escape I had had. They then decided that it would be a good idea if I tried to stand up, as they wanted to move me back to the German command post. With their aid I managed to get to my feet, and stood there like someone who has just put on skates for the first time. I didn't like to try to move in case I found I could not. However, I soon discovered that I was more or less intact, and that with the aid of a couple of Germans I could make slow progress down the road. The German command post was about half a mile away, but the walk seemed more like five miles. My leg and arm were very painful and I still felt very sick, but after a funereal procession lasting half an hour, we reached the post, which was situated in a small, white farmhouse.

Inside, three young German officers were standing over a German soldier who was decoding messages from a wireless set. One of the officers, an Austrian who spoke excellent English, pointed to a bench and told me to sit down. He then went to a cupboard from which he produced an American Red Cross outfit.

'Take off all your clothes and I will patch you up before sending you back to the dressing station. I understand you have had a very lucky escape. I am no doctor, but I will do my best.'

With these words he started to delve into the Red Cross box, which appeared to contain the very best equipment. I took off all my clothes and stood naked before him while the other two officers walked round me to examine the damage.

This examination showed that I had a hole through the right thigh and another through the top of my right arm; there were two small splinters in my back and one in the back of my head, and the joint bone was visible in my left wrist. Under the circumstances I had got off very lightly. The German officer patched the wounds and told me to dress again. While I was dressing, he talked to me and made a remark which I have heard several times since:

'What a tragedy that we are fighting against each other! We should be fighting together.'

I replied that I thought it was a great pity that anyone was fighting at all. He answered:

'Why do the English want to fight on Christmas Day? Why can you not let us enjoy our Christmas in peace? If you had not attacked on Christmas Eve, we should not have had to fight today. I cannot understand you.'

I pointed out to him that I was not responsible for fixing the days on which the British Army went into action. Looking round the room, I noticed that it was hung with evergreen Christmas decorations. The Germans certainly take their Christmas seriously! This farm was only a mile from the fighting line, and further back, where I stopped at a dressing station, the decorations were even more elaborate. Later that evening, in Tunis hospital, I met an American officer who told me that the German Tiger tank that picked him up after he was wounded had two miniature Christmas trees mounted on either side of the turret!

I sat at the command post for half an hour until a German staff car arrived on the scene. A very fat officer got out, his neck bulging over the back of his collar in typical Prussian style. He announced that he would be returning via the dressing station and that he would take me with him. The Austrian officer who had patched me up helped me into the car, and when I thanked him for all he had done, he said:

'I only hope that your people treat German officer prisoners as well as we have treated you.'

The fat staff officer, who was just getting into the driving seat, turned round and snapped:

'Of course they don't.'

He slammed the door. It looked as if our drive was not going to be a very conversational one, so I sat back and went to sleep. I awoke when the car stopped outside a large farm, where my fat conductor told me to get out. A medical orderly took me to the stables and told me to lie down in the straw.

After sleeping for three hours I was awakened by an orderly who told me that there was a truck outside which was going to take me to Tunis. I could not help smiling when I heard this. Our divisional commander had visited us a few days before and had assured us that we should be in Tunis on Christmas Day. I, at least, was working up to schedule.

The drive to Tunis did not take long. I noticed several burnt-out American tanks by the side of the road, which gave one an indication of how near to Tunis the Americans had got in the initial advance.

Our truck drew up in front of a big hospital, which had been taken over by the Germans, and I was helped out by the driver who conducted me to the hospital orderly room. An interpreter was sent for and all my particulars were written down on a special form, which was then handed to me. Everything was conducted in a most efficient style, with much clicking of heels and saluting as orderlies came in and out. I noticed that very few of them said *'Heil Hitler'* as they gave the Nazi salute.

The business in the orderly room was soon over, whereupon the interpreter asked me if I could walk to the operating theatre. I said that I could manage if he did not go too fast. We made our way down the passage, at the end of which was the operating theatre. There were already several wounded outside the door, some on stretchers, some sitting on benches. They were all Germans, except for one American soldier who looked as miserable as I felt.

The wait seemed endless. I was terribly tired and my wounds were feeling most uncomfortable. I longed to get to bed and sleep for a week. At last the door opened and I was told to go inside.

The sight that met my eyes made me want to run out again. There was a long operating table in the middle of the room with two arc lamps suspended over it. On either side of the table stood two men wearing red rubber aprons that were smeared with blood. The floor was littered with cast-off and bloody dressings, which a dirty old Arab was attempting to sweep into a corner. A clerk was sitting at a desk by the window and two German doctors were standing waiting for the next victim.

The men in the rubber aprons took off my clothes, a process which seemed to take only a few seconds. The next thing I knew I was lying face downwards on the operating table, while one of the aproned orderlies removed the dressings and another stuck an anti-tetanus injection into my leg. The doctors then advanced on the scene, and while they examined the damage they called out details which were repeated and written down on my sheet by the clerk in the corner of the room. I was very soon cleaned up and comfortably bandaged. My clothes were put on me by the orderlies and I was wheeled out of the theatre. The interpreter, who was waiting outside, then had me carried off to a ward.

The hospital was very full, so the Germans had built several outside wards consisting of long wooden huts divided into two, with twenty beds in each partition. I was taken to one of these wards where I was handed over to an American stretcher bearer called Samuel Lokich, a native of Long Island.

The interior of the ward presented a magnificent spectacle. In the middle of the room was a long table which had a five-foot high Christmas tree rising majestically from its centre. The tree was beautifully decorated with silver snow, coloured lights and other ornaments. I was told later that every other ward was similarly decorated. The inmates of the ward were Germans, Americans and a few English. I was the only officer in the ward when I arrived, but later that evening a young American officer was brought in. Samuel Lokich was a tower of strength. He had the whole place 'taped', and he seemed to be on very good terms with the German authorities.

It was shortly after 6 p.m. when I was brought into the ward, and the patients had just finished their Christmas supper. Sam took me to a bed, fixed me up with blankets and said that he would return shortly with some seasonal fare. I suddenly realized that I had had nothing to eat for twenty-four hours and was extremely hungry. Sam soon returned with a plate full of German sausage, bread, butter, jam and hot coffee. The food was delicious and the coffee, though ersatz, was good.

There was a German soldier in the bed opposite me. He watched me with interest while I ate my meal, and when he saw me start to drink my coffee he got up and came over to me with a bottle in his hand. He asked me if I would like some brandy in my coffee. This seemed to me an excellent idea, so I said 'Yes, please' in my very best German. The soldier insisted on filling the mug to the top, assuring me that he did not like the stuff himself. He told me that every German in the hospital had been given a bottle of brandy for Christmas.

The mixture of coffee and brandy was excellent, and had a most soporific effect. Once in bed I felt that I should like to stay there for ever.

Before I went to sleep two guardsmen from my company were brought into the ward. One was badly wounded, the other very slightly. They were both so tired and dazed that it was difficult to find out any news of the rest of the battalion from them. I think they felt as I did – that the only thing worth doing was to sleep and sleep and sleep.

I was awakened after a few hours by a terrific barrage of anti-aircraft guns, which seemed to be firing just outside the window. The whole ward shook and I could hear the crunch of the bombs falling in the distance. The RAF was paying its nightly visit to the port of Tunis. Nobody seemed to pay much attention, and I very soon went off to sleep again.

When I awoke the next morning I could not remember where I was. A twinge from my leg, however, very soon brought me back to my senses; now I was thoroughly rested, the wretchedness of my situation began to dawn upon me. The previous evening I had been too tired to care or think, but now there was no evading it. I was a prisoner of war in German hands and would probably remain so for two years. But supposing the war went on for another four years, or even five! The more I thought about it, the more depressed I became. It had never entered my head that I would be taken prisoner. I had always felt that that was something that happened to other people but would never happen to me.

Arab orderlies swept the room and German soldiers brought in our breakfast of brown bread, butter, jam and black coffee. There was an old Arab in the bed next to me who had been injured in an air raid. The Germans were making a great fuss of him, presumably for propaganda purposes. He was a revolting creature and smelt extremely high.

The German patients in the ward were for the most part very young boys, some of whom were slightly wounded, and others resting. Although young, they were all veterans, having seen service in Austria, Poland, France and Russia. They all admitted that fighting in Russia was no picnic. One of them said:

'You can shoot a Russian's legs off, and then his arms, but he will manage to go on firing his machine-gun.'

One young fellow of eighteen, who had seen two years' service in a Panzer regiment, used to go shopping on our behalf. We pooled all our money, giving it to Sam, who sent the young German into the town to buy necessities such as toothbrushes, razors and soap.

I talked quite a lot with the young German soldiers. Their morale was very high at that time, and they were absolutely certain that they were going to win the war. When I told them that I was equally certain the Allies were going to win, they roared with laughter. However, they assured me that it was only right that I should think so, otherwise I would not be a good soldier. They were convinced that the Germans would finish the Russians off that summer (1943) and then turn all their attention to the war against England.

At lunch on my second day in hospital I was told that a German intelligence officer was coming to question me that afternoon. I immediately pictured some terrifying Nazi from the SS with third degree methods. I determined only to give him my name, rank and number. We had had it drilled into us at home that on no account were we to say any more. I was having my tea when in walked an elderly officer, wearing *pince-nez* and looking rather like a benevolent schoolmaster. He introduced himself and asked when it would be convenient for him to question me. I suggested that we might get down to it at once, but he insisted that I should first finish my tea.

This I did, and then he came over, sat on my bed and handed me a packet of English cigarettes. An Austrian, he spoke perfect English, having spent many years in London.

'I dislike this job intensely, Captain Kindersley,' he said, 'so we will get it over as quickly as possible. As a matter of fact there is very little I want to ask you, as I already know your regiment, battalion, brigade, when you left England and what training you were doing before you sailed. So you see, there is not much more to know. But, tell me, what do you think of the Americans?'

I was so astonished by this unexpected method of approach that it took me some time to reply.

'From what I have seen of them I think they are very good. What do you think of the Russians?'

For a moment I thought I had been rather unwise to poke this question at him, but he only smiled and said:

'I have recently returned from Russia. The fighting there is terrible and the cold beyond belief. The Russians fight like savages.'

I thought he might be bluffing about the details that he professed to know about me, so I asked him to enlarge on them.

He not only knew all the details, but also the names of the commanding officer and company commanders when we left England. He told me about the combined operations training which we had done at Inverary, actually giving me the dates and the names of the ships we were on. The only mistake he made was when he told me that my commanding officer had been killed; in fact he had only been wounded.

Before leaving, my questioner asked if there was anything he could do for me. I was most anxious that my period of being posted missing should be as short as possible, so I asked him if he could expedite my name being sent through the Red Cross. He took particulars of my name and number and promised to do all he could, saying that he might get it sent over the radio. (I learned later that he had failed, as I was posted missing for seven weeks.)

After I had been in Tunis hospital for three days the German doctor certified me fit for travel and I was informed that I should be leaving by air for Germany the following morning. The young American officer, Paul Carnes, was scheduled to travel with me. Paul and I were to see a lot of each other during the next three months. He had been badly wounded in the foot and also had a bullet through his knee.

At nine o'clock the next morning, the ambulance arrived outside the ward and we gathered our few belongings together ready to leave. Two other American soldiers and one German were also travelling with us. One of the Americans, Healey by name, had a very bad wound in the shoulder. He was one of the toughest men I have ever met; no pain was too much for him. The other American was only slightly wounded, but the German had very severe burns on the face which had been covered with grease, giving him a terrible appearance.

We were helped into the ambulance by Sam and were soon rattling off towards Tunis airport, which lay just to the right of the city. It was a hot day and the atmosphere inside the ambulance was very stuffy. The German travelled in a different ambulance from us. Our driver stopped on the road by the side of the airfield, but we were told that as the aeroplane had not yet arrived we might have to wait an hour or so. The atmosphere inside the ambulance became worse and worse and it was not improved by the innumerable cigarettes that were smoked. After about an hour we heard a roar of engines and saw through the window seventeen Junkers 52s circling overhead. Our driver immediately started up his engine and drove us onto the airfield, stopping opposite what had once been the civilian booking office. The aeroplanes landed one by one and taxied to different parts of the field. Our papers were handed to a German officer, who immediately told our driver which plane to take us to. No time was wasted and our ambulance soon drew up alongside one of the big three-engined planes, which were already being unloaded of their freight.

While we were waiting to get in, we had a chance to look at the airport. In the far corner there were the remains of the hangars, which had been blasted by the RAF. By the side of this mass of rubble there was a considerable pile of wrecked German planes. The field itself had been badly bombed and a large number of Arabs were filling in the craters with earth. Red flags denoted particularly bad patches – these were no numerous that it must have been extremely difficult for the pilots to find a clear run. While the fleet of Junkers 52s were on the ground, an umbrella of Messerschmitts roared overhead waiting to drive off the Spitfires that were constantly prowling about the district. The sight of the Messerschmitts reminded us, if we needed any reminding, what a hazardous journey we were about to embark on. Before my capture I had constantly heard of the number of German transport planes that the RAF was destroying daily between Tunis and Italy. Here we were, on a perfect flying day for fighters, waiting to fly over this dangerous stretch of sea.

We were just discussing the unpleasantness of our situation when we were hustled into the plane. There were no seats, so we had to lie or sit on the floor. Carnes and Healey were lifted into the plane, while the other American, the burned German and myself scrambled in as best we could. The engines were started up, we were each given a yellow life-jacket, the solitary rear gunner took up his position, and the plane started to ready for take-off. Our plane must have been very ancient, as it rattled and shook in the most alarming manner as it taxied across the very rough surface of the

19

airport. We soon gathered speed and were airborne after one last and violent bump. I sat up and peered out of the window, watching the other planes take off one by one.

Our pilot steered straight out to sea but never went higher than two hundred feet. The fighter cover left us once we were over the sea, and the whole fleet of Junkers got into close formation at a height of about a hundred feet above the water. Every moment we expected to hear the scream of a Spitfire, in which case it was reasonable to assume that we were for 'the high jump'. The noise inside the plane was terrific, making it impossible to talk. Paul Carnes had never been in an aeroplane before; it certainly was not a very pleasant introduction to flying. The further out to sea we went, the less was our danger, as in those days the fighters' range was limited.

After an hour and a quarter, we sighted Sicily. On reaching the coast, we turned left and flew along the west coast, finally cutting across to Palermo. We circled over the town for some time and then landed at the very small, cramped airport. We had no idea why we were coming down, as we had been told that we were flying direct to Naples *en route* for Germany. Only six of our convoy landed at Palermo, the rest going on towards Italy. Our plane taxied over to the edge of the airfield and the pilot switched off the engines. As the rear gunner got out, he told us that we were stopping there for half an hour and that we could get out if we wanted to. We all managed to get out of the plane, and sat on the grass smoking cigarettes and heaving sighs of relief at having come safely through the fighter area.

Palermo aerodrome had been completely taken over by the Germans. With the exception of a few mechanics, there were no Italians in sight. I had yet to meet an Italian soldier, as we had seen none in Tunisia. While we were waiting at Palermo we saw the huge Dornier troop-carrying planes which the Germans were then using between Italy and Tunis. These planes had six engines, ten wheels and the largest wing span I had ever seen on any aeroplane. The fuselage was very deep in front but tapered off to a narrow tail. In the front of the fuselage were two decks, the top one being occupied by the pilots. These planes could carry a light tank, an artillery piece or seventy-five men. When in flight in the distance the Dornier resembled a huge bat. Although they had several machine-guns jutting out at various points, they were easy meat for a fighter, as their top speed was not high.

Our plane took off again, but instead of heading northwards, as we had expected, it clung to the coast of Sicily until it reached the northern end of the Straits of Messina, where it turned south. In a few moments we had passed over the town of Messina and were crossing the narrow straits towards a small aerodrome on the mainland, which turned out to be Reggio Calabria. We circled over the town and then landed. This was our destination. Why we went to Reggio Calabria, I never discovered. All the other planes went elsewhere, and very few other prisoners came to Reggio Calabria after us. I suppose it was just the luck of the draw.

2

Reggio Calabria

The aerodrome at Reggio Calabria had been taken over by the Germans, but there were several Italian fighter planes on the ground. The Italian fighter planes then flew above the aerodrome executing some daring aerobatics – a form of amusement they did not indulge in when any of our planes visited the locality during the next three months.

An ambulance drew up alongside our plane, into which were put Paul Carnes and the German. Healey, myself and the other American (I cannot remember his name) were taken over to an office on the outskirts of the aerodrome. It was here that I came across the first typical Nazi I had met since my capture. Up to this time most of the Germans we had seen had been quite harmless people, against whom it was difficult to work up a hate, but in the airport office at Reggio I saw two Nazis whom I shall not forget in a hurry. They were both pilots in the *Luftwaffe*, very smart in their grey uniforms and well set-up caps, and as vain as a couple of peacocks. They looked at us as if we were so much dirt, and treated us accordingly.

Both Healey and I were very tired, and it must have been perfectly apparent to anyone that we were wounded. The German officers made us stand up, until finally both of us sat down on the floor regardless of their instructions. The other German soldiers seemed rather scared of these two officers, and whenever they came into the room there was much clicking of heels and 'heiling' of Hitler. After sitting on the floor for an hour, we were told to clear out. An ambulance was waiting outside the door to take us to hospital. Poor Healey was suffering a great deal. The wound in his shoulder was discharging very freely and the pus had soaked through his bandages and his coat. The smell was terrible, and no one disliked it more than Healey, who kept on swearing about 'my God-damned stink'.

Our ambulance was rather an ancient one, but the German driver seemed to be in a hurry and he managed to flog it along at a pretty good speed. We raced over the cobbled streets on the outskirts of

Reggio Calabria, our driver keeping his finger firmly pressed on a very shrill Italian-type hooter. After travelling about a mile, we drew up in a narrow street before a building that had a Red Cross sign on the door. Our driver opened the back doors of the ambulance but told us to remain where we were. Within a few seconds, the ambulance was surrounded by an excited mob of Italians, mostly women and children. They were all talking at once and pointing out to each other the '*inglesi*' and '*americani*'. We were all too tired to appreciate our audience and would soon have been rather rude to them if the German driver had not come to the rescue. He shouted '*Via, via!*', whereupon they scattered like a flock of frightened sheep.

Paul Carnes was then brought out of the building and put into our ambulance. He had been taken off by mistake to a German soldiers' hospital, where he had found himself quite alone with a crowd of wounded Germans. His relief at seeing us again was considerable.

The door of the ambulance was slammed again and we tore off at an ever-increasing speed through the streets of Reggio. Shortly after passing the station we turned sharp right up a steep hill, finally coming to a halt in front of a very impressive white stone building, approached by a double flight of white marble steps. The steps joined again on a terrace from which hung a mass of bougainvillea. As we hobbled up the steps a nun opened the front door.

I shall always remember the first time I saw her, standing there in her black dress and spotless white starched coif, welcoming us with outstretched arms. She was the kindest and most charming person I have ever met, and wherever she went the beastliness of war seemed to disappear.

Inside the door there was a small hall, with a flight of white stone steps leading to a landing with doors on either side of it. The steps continued on from the landing through a glass door to another floor.

We were taken through the door on the right of the landing into a ward about fifty feet long by twenty feet wide. It was a very cheerful room with light blue distempered walls, and contained twenty-six beds, all unoccupied. For some strange reason, Sister put the three Americans in beds at one end of the room and took me to a bed at the other end. Perhaps she thought that the Americans and English would fight if put together! We were each given a pair of blue and white check pyjamas and were told to get into bed. During this time

Sister Antonio had been most sympathetic about our wounds and assured us that we should be very happy and comfortable in the hospital. She repeatedly assured us that 'God will take care of everything'.

Sister had lived in America as a girl, but had left there some thirty years ago, with the result that she had forgotten most of her English. She had, however, a charming manner of speaking with a slight American accent. She told us that in this hospital the war must be forgotten. We were all brothers and must help each other.

'God will take care. God will take care.' How many times was I to hear her use these words, with her hands clasped and her eyes raised to heaven.

'The war, it ees teerrible. So much sadness, but God will take care.'

An Italian medical orderly soon arrived in the ward and was told by Sister to help us into bed, while she went to see about our supper. Our beds looked most inviting, as they had clean white sheets, something none of us had seen for some time. Our medical orderly, who was called Dominic, spoke no English, and as we spoke no Italian conversation was somewhat difficult. Dominic took it for granted that we understood Italian and talked to us incessantly while we were getting to bed. We managed to gather from his conversation that this was not a proper hospital, but a home for old men and women. The old folks had been banished to the top floor, while the remainder of the hospital had been taken over by the government as a military hospital.

The building was situated on a hill above Reggio Calabria and overlooked the Straits of Messina. On a clear day one could see the then snow-covered peak of Mount Etna rising majestically behind the coastal hills of Sicily.

We had not been in bed long before Sister appeared with our meal, which consisted of spaghetti, omelette, bread and a quarter litre of red wine. I don't think I have ever enjoyed a meal more. Naturally, we thought we had struck a really good hospital where we were going to enjoy excellent meals. Little did we know what was in store for us in that direction!

Sister stayed and talked to us while we ate our supper, asking us many questions regarding our families, wives and children. She asked if any of us were Catholics. Healey was the only one, but it made no difference to Sister, who remarked that a good Protestant was better than a bad Catholic.

Before we went to sleep the first night we were washed by Dominic, who informed us that we should have 'medication' the next morning. 'Medication' meant a visit to the operating theatre. I had not had my dressings changed for three days and they were extremely uncomfortable. Poor Healey was in a very bad state, but a comfortable bed with clean sheets made up for everything. I felt very isolated up my end of the ward, and was forced to shout in order to carry on a conversation with the others.

We all slept very well that night. We were awakened the next morning by Dominic, who washed us and then swept and cleaned the ward. Breakfast consisted of a cup of coffee and an orange and we were told that the medication would start at nine o'clock.

Sister came in after breakfast, bringing with her two Italian Red Cross women, smartly dressed in white with a large red cross on their bosoms. One of them, Signora Verducci, was the local school-mistress, the other was a young, dark, Jewish-looking Italian girl. Verducci was short, stout and efficient. She wore *pince-nez* and acted as a sort of chaperon to the younger Red Cross girls. Some days she would bring two girls with her, changing them around so that they each attended about four days a week. Their job was to wash us, make the beds and attend medication. This was at times rather embarrassing, but we soon got accustomed to it. Verducci spoke a certain amount of French, which enabled us to converse together daily.

We did not start off very well, for when I told her that I was not a Catholic she called me a heathen, which I naturally rather resented. We followed this up by having an argument about the war, which, she informed me, Italy had entered into for reasons of justice! However, we soon managed to get on to pleasanter subjects and in the end we became good friends. Verducci was a hard worker and had a kind heart.

Paul Carnes, who had been moved into the bed next to me first thing in the morning, proved a great attraction to the younger Red Cross nurse. She never left him in peace, always wanting to brush his hair or manicure his nails. At times she drove him crazy. Even if he pretended to be asleep, she would come over and pull his hair.

At 9 a.m. I was put on a stretcher and wheeled off to the medication room by Dominic, with Verducci and her assistant in attendance. There were two Italian doctors in the operating theatre, one a charming old major with very broad shoulders and a square grey beard, and the other a pompous and fat little major, whose only claim to being a doctor lay in the fact that he carried a stethoscope which, incidentally, he never used. Both doctors wore white coats over their uniforms. The old major pulled off my sticky dressings as painlessly as possible and examined the damage. The small wounds in my back and head were practically healed, but my leg, arm and wrist were in rather a mess. These he bandaged up with masses of cotton wool, a commodity of which there appeared to be no shortage in Italy. The young VAD wrote down details on my hospital sheet, while Verducci assisted the old major. The fat and pompous creature, whom we later nicknamed 'Musso', stood and looked on in a manner which suggested that his presence was absolutely essential. During the three months that I was at Reggio, I never saw him do one thing which might suggest that he was a doctor.

The old major was always most kind to us, buying us countless cigarettes which he paid for out of his own pocket. He also spoke a certain amount of French, so I acted as general interpreter between him and the patients. Sister told us that he was an anti-Fascist and did not get on very well with the other officers. This fact, unfortunately for us, led to his removal after a few weeks.

When I got back from medication some other patients from the floor above had been brought down to our ward. There was one French officer, called Jacques Massué, three French and four English soldiers. Jacques Massué had been badly wounded in the leg, but the other Frenchmen were only slightly wounded. Three of the English were pretty badly knocked about. One of them, Smith, an old soldier of eleven years' service, had a broken leg, which was suspended in a kind of cradle with weights attached to it. Smith was a most cheerful soul, of the true Cockney type. He suffered a great deal, but was always smiling and was a great favourite with Sister and the VADs. One of the Frenchmen, a marine, had tried to escape from Vichy-controlled North Africa before the arrival of our troops. He was very bitter about Vichy France and his one ambition was to join the British Navy or Merchant Navy. Unfortunately he could not speak a word of English, so I agreed to give him two hours of lessons each day – an arrangement that greatly helped to pass the time and also improved my French.

The date was now 30 December. The other patients had already been in hospital for a fortnight, so we were able to find out from them what was in store for us. I am afraid that our first inquiry was about the food! Their information on this subject was most depressing. The daily menu was as follows:

8 a.m. Coffee

Midday Small bowl of very liquid spaghetti with a slice of horse flesh floating in it

4.30 p.m. Small bowl of rice

In addition, we had two rolls each day, one orange and a quarter-litre of red wine. There were no Red Cross parcels and no cigarettes. The hospital was presumably not known of at Geneva, so we never received the parcels that most other hospitals and camps were getting once a week.

The diet seemed to us akin to starvation, and the wait from 4.30 p.m. to noon the next day was very testing. There was, however, one bright spot. Sister had made it known in the town that there were wounded prisoners at the hospital and that visitors would be welcomed. Her appeal was not in vain, and we had numerous visitors on Saturdays and Sundays, all of whom brought us food or cigarettes. Food was not plentiful in Reggio Calabria, but I shall never forget the kindness and generosity of the Italian civilians in the town. They treated us as friends; we found it difficult to believe that these were our enemies, and were being repeatedly bombed by our planes. I have no regard for Fascists or the Italian army, but nowhere in the world would you find kinder or more generous people than the Italians. I wondered at this kindness in Reggio Calabria, but I was to wonder at it even more when, seven months later, I walked four hundred miles through Italy, entirely dependent on Italian hospitality.

The patients who had been in the hospital over Christmas told us that the Italian Red Cross, together with the civilians, had supplied them with a wonderful meal and that this would be repeated on New Year's Day, which is celebrated in a big way in Italy. On any important saint's day we also had a good chance of getting a lot of extras, so we all hastily scanned the calendar in order to figure out which saints would prove to be our own particular saviours.

New Year's Day arrived. Sister came into the ward as usual in the morning, but we could tell by her delighted expression that something good was in store for us. We were not to be disappointed; on the stroke of noon the doors were thrown open and in marched an impressive array of females, dressed in various uniforms. They were led by an enormous creature sporting a blue uniform with white facings. Her hair was coal black and curly, while her face was made up in such a way that it reminded one of the sunsets over Sicily. On entering the room she gave the Fascist salute and shouted: '*Comè sta?*' (How are you?) She was followed by others in similar uniform; they were carrying two large aluminium containers, from which exuded the most delicious aroma. The rear of the party was brought up by Red Cross girls, bearing gifts of cakes, oranges, sweets and cigarettes. Last of all came Sister, her face wreathed in smiles, as it always was when she saw we were pleased. Paul Carnes and I sat up in bed with our eyes popping and our mouths watering. We were each given an enormous helping of really well cooked spaghetti with tomato sauce. Those who wanted it had a second helping – I certainly did not hold back! There followed a generous plateful of chicken and fried potatoes and, finally, the cakes, sweets and oranges. In the meantime, an Italian orderly poured out large glasses of excellent red wine, which this galaxy of Italian femininity had brought. A very pretty girl of about seventeen then handed us cigarettes, and she also gave me an English book. During the meal the two heads of the local Red Cross organization came into the ward. One, a *marchesa*, was head of the provincial Red Cross, and the other, a *contessa*, head of the Reggio Calabria branch. They were both very charming ladies and both talked French.

That night, ten more patients arrived, including three Frenchmen. One, a sergeant, had been severely wounded. His legs were badly smashed and he had a ghastly wound in his hip. He was put in the bed next to Paul Carnes, one away from me. His leg was put into a similar contraption to Smith's, which made it imperative that he should keep still. The Germans had covered his hip in plaster of Paris, but the Italian doctor took this off. I have never seen such a wound, nor have I ever smelt anything like the stink that came from it. The poor man was in dreadful pain, and it was very soon apparent that he could not take it. He could not bear his leg being in the cradle and was constantly trying to move it. I went over and talked to him before we went to sleep that night and told him that it was essential for his recovery that he keep still.

Unfortunately, he discovered that the one time he could get the weights taken off was when he sat on the bedpan. The result was that he cried for the bedpan every half hour during the night. Poor Dominic, who worked like a slave for us day and night, had to keep on getting out of bed (he slept in the ward) to put the unfortunate Frenchman on the bedpan. This went on all through the night.

I got out of bed several times to try and persuade him to keep still, and Dominic gave him two injections. However, nothing did any good and he continued to rave and shout for the bedpan. Eventually, at about three in the morning, Dominic's patience gave out. He seized the bedpan from under the startled patient and advanced towards my bed, waving this familiar hospital utensil above his head and shouting in Italian:

'Eleven times have I given him the pan, eleven times he does nothing – this cannot go on.'

I could not help laughing, although I felt desperately sorry for the Frenchman. The poor fellow went to sleep at about 5 a.m. from sheer exhaustion, but it was apparent the next morning that his end was near. The Italian doctor did all he could but the constant movement caused incessant loss of blood from the hip. A priest was sent for that afternoon and the Frenchman died the next night. I think it was a happy release. Two days later the Italians accorded him a full military funeral.

On our second day in hospital we were visited by a Jesuit priest, who brought with him a young American who was undergoing his fifteen years' study at the Jesuit College prior to becoming a priest. He had already done seven years and had begun to forget his native tongue. The elder priest was a very pleasant man. He spoke fluent French and we had many interesting talks together during the next three months. The young American priest-to-be, although very kind, was rather tiresome at first, as he would try and convert us all to Catholicism. Our first conversation together was somewhat peculiar and ran something like this:

'Are you a Catholic?'

'No.'

'Why don't you believe in Jesus Christ?'

'I do.'

'No you don't.'

'I beg your pardon, but I do.'

'Oh, no you don't.'

And so on. Eventually I gave up, but I never discovered why he thought I did not believe in Jesus Christ.

The Jesuit priests were very good to us, bringing cigarettes, chestnuts and oranges. Anyone who brought us food could be forgiven anything! This sounds rather a crude method of assessing people, but when one has to live on Italian hospital rations one's sense of values becomes somewhat distorted.

One amusing incident occurred in connection with the priests. Smith, the old soldier, was a heavy smoker, and was willing to sell his soul for cigarettes. After weighing up the situation for several weeks, he came to the conclusion that he would get more cigarettes out of the visitors if he was a Catholic. He therefore agreed with the young priest to turn Catholic. The priest was naturally delighted and agreed to introduce him to the mysteries of the Catholic Church during the next month, prior to his official entry into the bosom of Rome. By this time I had been moved into another ward, but I happened to hear of Smith's religious activities. As senior British officer in the hospital, I felt that I should do something about it in case Smith was married and had children who were Protestants. I went down to see Smith in order to make sure that he realized the seriousness of the step he was taking, but he told me that he was not married and, as far as he knew, had no relations.

'I have got no religion,' he said, 'and so I might just as well be a Catholic.'

There was nothing more to be said, so Smith continued with his conversion, his bed table being covered with emblems and pictures of the Catholic faith which, he assured me, had already brought in good results in the cigarette line. As luck would have it, just before his baptism he was sent to a permanent camp, where cigarettes were provided by the British Red Cross.

By 2 January our ward was beginning to fill up. An Irish officer, Captain Walter Grant, had arrived with several other ranks. Among the latter was a guardsman from my battalion called Stewart. He had a bad wound in the head which had paralysed the whole of his left side. He suffered very little pain, but was, of course, completely helpless. He was always very cheerful, and whenever I asked him how he felt, he always used to answer: 'Champion, sir.' When I left the hospital three months later, he was just beginning to get some feeling in his left side. There was another soldier with a paralysed side. He suffered a great deal but his recovery was quicker than Stewart's. The faithful Dominic was particularly kind and gentle with these two men, and would get out of his bed at all hours of the night to move them into a more comfortable position.

None of us slept very well in the big ward because there was nearly always someone groaning with pain, and when the patients were silent the guards used to keep us awake. Although only three or four of us could walk, we had three guards in the ward day and night. They were the lowest type of Italian soldier – which, believe me, is as low as you can find anywhere. They used to play cards all night at a table in the middle of the ward and made no effort to talk quietly.

I was just getting very fed up with the ward and all its inmates, when Sister made a wonderful suggestion. She asked me if the four officers – Paul Carnes, Walter Grant, Jacques Massué and myself – would like to move into a smaller ward by ourselves. Naturally, we jumped at the offer, and that afternoon we were moved upstairs into a room of our own. The room had its disadvantages, but it was worth a lot to get away from the big ward. One of the chief disadvantages was that it looked out into the street. In a small house opposite there was a very ancient gramophone, which played the same three records day and night for three months. One of these tunes was the famous German marching song 'Lili Marlene', a great favourite with German and Italian troops.

We had two special guards to look after us, and in these we were extremely lucky. Their names were Vincenzo and Francesco. Vincenzo was a very cheerful and generous person. We could always rely on him for chestnuts and cigarettes. He was sick of the war and definitely anti-Fascist. Francesco was a really good fellow. His home was in Trieste and he was much more Slav than Italian. He was an ardent anti-Fascist and was openly pro-British in all his sentiments. Whenever he spoke of Mussolini he spat on the floor. A born optimist, he assured us that Britain would win the war within three months. We had additional guards, but one of these two was usually in attendance. The guards, incidentally, were entirely for my benefit, as none of the other three officers could walk at all; even I could only hobble at the beginning, but I was not even allowed to go to the lavatory without a guard accompanying me.

The days in Reggio Calabrio hospital passed terribly slowly, as we had absolutely nothing to do. As I have already mentioned, the hospital was not under the wing of Geneva, so we had no books or games to help pass the time. We therefore had to rely almost entirely on conversation, which naturally rather dried up after three months. The only English book we had was one brought by the Jesuit priest entitled *The Life of the Virgin Mary*. We each read this book several times, and at the end of three months there was nothing we did not know on this interesting subject.

I taught the others the old game of 'battleships' – a pastime not unknown on the London Stock Exchange in times of depression. All you require for this somewhat infantile game is a piece of paper and a pencil. As paper was rather short, every available piece was used, including my diary. (This had an amusing sequel when I went to a permanent camp. The Italians, searching me in the usual manner, found my diary, which was full of little squares with numbers on them. These they took to represent a code, so my diary was sent off to the intelligence staff in Rome, who tried to decipher it. It was eventually returned to me after three weeks. I often wonder what they made of it all.)

When we were not playing battleships or reading about the Virgin Mary we used to sit up in bed and talk while the infernal gramophone on the other side of the street blared out its three well-worn tunes.

As we got better, so our appetites increased, and at times we felt like eating the sheets. In the evening, with another seventeen hours before the next meal, we used to think out menus of the kind of dinner we should like most. Paul always went for ice creams and cherry pie and Grant and I for a mixed grill at Simpson's.

Our extreme hunger was greatly helped by Sister. Once we had got a room to ourselves she used to come and see us a great deal. Her kindness was quite phenomenal. Every day, regardless of the weather, she would walk down the long hill into the town and buy us figs, chestnuts, oranges and other delicacies. We had no money, so it all had to come out of her own pocket. At six o'clock in the evening she would slip into the ward and produce, out of a remarkable pocket in her dress, her purchases of the day. Sometimes a bottle of wine would also appear from this pocket, which seemed to be of unfathomable depth. She would then share the food out among us, and sit on a stool and talk to us while we ate. In answer to our thanks, she would merely say: 'It is nothing,' and we could see the great pleasure she took in giving. If someone were to ask me what I mean by a good Christian, I would introduce him to Sister Antonio.

If any of the prisoners downstairs were suffering, she would always manage to get them milk or an egg beaten up in wine. She was certainly the Florence Nightingale of Reggio Calabria. An ardent anti-Fascist, she used to talk to us a lot of Mussolini and Hitler, whom she described as 'those devils'. She told us that there was much unrest in the town and prophesied that there would be a political revolution in Italy within six months – a very accurate forecast. Once a week she would go to a friend's house and listen to the BBC, bringing us back a full report. This used to worry us, as we felt she might get caught. But she had no fear of anyone, Fascist or otherwise. There was only one thing that frightened her: the air raids, which took place regularly three or four times a week. We could see the planes from our window, and there was an anti-aircraft battery not far from the hospital, which used to shake with the noise of bombs and gunfire. Sometimes Sister would come into our ward during these raids. When she heard the guns or the bombs she would clasp her hands and pray to all the saints in heaven. We did our best to calm her, but she could never get used to it.

The raids had two very unfortunate sequels for us. The first was when some civilian dwellings were hit, killing many people. The civilian hospital was packed to overflowing, so a ward in our hospital was put at their disposal. One afternoon a poor Italian woman was brought in whose husband and three children had been killed that afternoon. Her fourth child, a little girl, was also wounded. We heard the cries of this unfortunate woman and her child for three days and nights. As the bombing was usually done by American planes, poor Carnes used to get all the blame for the raids, as if he had ordered them himself.

The other sequel to the raids was really a disaster for us all. One afternoon, our friend the *marchesa* gave a large party for the archbishop of Calabria. This was attended by all the important people in Reggio, both civil and military, and a large number of military cars were parked outside the *marchesa*'s house. Our bombers came over that afternoon and, seeing a lot of cars parked around a large house, they probably thought it was a military head-quarters. Two planes zoomed down and dropped a stick of bombs across the house, killing the *marchesa*, her husband and two daughters, and blowing the archbishop's head off.

This was an appalling catastrophe and naturally incensed the whole population. Once again, poor Paul Carnes came in for all the blame. One might have thought that he himself had beheaded the unfortunate archbishop. The next morning Signora Verducci burst into the ward, her eyes red with weeping, and called us all a pack of murderers. Nothing we could say would calm her and she soon rushed out of the ward, slamming the door behind her. We did not see her again for three weeks.

Sister alone remained perfectly calm and explained to everyone that it was not our fault and that it was just the misfortune of war. It was, however, a very embarrassing situation for us. We sent a message to the *contessa* expressing our sincere regret for what had happened. Naturally, our stock of delicacies slumped, and visitors were scarce for the next week.

We had Sister to thank for all our visitors. It was she who arranged for them to come and it was she who suggested that they bring food. On Saturdays and Sundays we would have as many as thirty or forty visitors. Occasionally, an entire Catholic girls' school would arrive, escorted by nuns. Above each of our beds was a square black board, on which was written our name, nationality, age, place of birth, particulars of wounds and rank. Our visitors used to stand at the end of our beds reading aloud our particulars. It was rather embarrassing, especially as our knowledge of Italian was practically nil. We had no one to teach us and no books to learn from. Paul Carnes always attracted the most attention, being the *americano* of the party. When our visitors read that he came from Indiana, they were surprised that he did not have brown skin and a feathered head-dress. On one point they were all agreed: he must be very rich, as in Italian eyes all Americans are millionaires.

After the bombing of the archbishop, Signora Verducci practically disappeared from our lives. Her place was taken by the stationmaster's wife. She was a magnificent woman, tall and stout, with a very deep voice, and she was exceptionally efficient. Everyone called her 'Mamma'. Her assistant and companion was an extremely pretty VAD called Anita. Unfortunately, she could not speak a word of English or French, so conversation was rather limited. But we got on very well.

Since we had been moved into our upstairs ward, we did not have to go down for medication; the Italian doctors came up to our room to do the dressings, assisted by Mamma, Anita and the Italian medical sergeant. The latter had a most distressing habit of smoking a cheroot in a holder while he was doing our dressings, and there would always be about a quarter of an inch of ash hanging perilously over our open wounds. Mamma, though efficient, was quite without mercy when pulling off dressings or plaster. A snip of her scissors, a sharp tug and off would come an extremely adhesive dressing, much to the discomfort of the patient. Anita was the exact opposite, quiet and gentle. When Mamma, Anita and the sergeant entered the ward there was great competition to see who could get

Anita's services. I think that Jacques Massué usually came off best as he could speak a little Italian.

Despite good treatment by all in the hospital, our rate of recovery was terribly slow. Our wounds simply refused to heal and this we attributed to the diet from which nutritive food was lacking. My own wounds, which were comparatively slight, would have healed completely in a month on a normal diet. As it was it took three months for me to get well.

After three weeks, the old Italian doctor was sent on leave, from which he never returned. Sister informed us that he did not get on well with the rest of the staff, who were more Fascist in their tendencies than he. He was replaced by a very ancient doctor, who had been recalled from retirement to rejoin the military medical staff. He must have been seventy if he was a day, and his hands shook in the most alarming manner. What little hair he had was as white as snow and his shoulders were bent with age. A pair of steel-rimmed spectacles balanced on the end of his nose, though I noticed that he always looked over and not through them. We inquired anxiously of Sister regarding his medical capacity, and were told that he had been a very good surgeon years ago and that he was very kind. There was no doubt that he knew his stuff, but he had only one cure for every ailment – the knife, and a very sharp one at that!

I was the first of the four of us to fall under the doctor's knife. My leg, which had nearly healed, suddenly started to swell. The next morning the doctor looked at it over his glasses, mentioned the word *coltello* and pattered out of the room with a delighted expression on his face. Before his return Mamma told me my fate – the doctor was going to have a dig to find the offending piece of shrapnel. The other three sat up in their beds to watch the fun. Back came the old gentleman with his surgeon's knife, a syringe and a bottle of freezing mixture. He was wearing his military cap, which he seemed to regard as an essential part of his equipment. Everything was prepared, my bandages were taken off and the old doctor stuck the rather blunt syringe into my leg. I never discovered whether this was supposed to be a local anaesthetic, but whatever it was, it had no effect whatsoever. When I saw the doctor advancing with his knife, I clutched hold of the bars of the bed and raised my eyes to heaven. With shaking hands, the old man proceeded to make a deep incision about three inches long in my leg. This done, he put his thumb in one end and ran it the length of the incision. By this time I was groaning with pain and wriggling about like a fish on a slab, much to the annoyance of the sergeant, who was holding me down, his cigar still in his mouth. The doctor then poured some freezing mixture into the incision, preparatory to having another search. This was even more painful than the first time, but was, however, successful, the old man extracting the offending, microscopic, piece of shrapnel. As he removed his thumb, I wrenched my arms free and accidently knocked his hat off.

He was delighted with his morning's work and proceeded to put strapping across the incision he had made. Stitches were no good as the wound had to be left open. Paul, Walter and Jacques had enjoyed a front-row seat for this operation and were most sympathetic to me as I lay perspiring on the bed. Little did they know what was in store for them in the near future! Within a week Paul's foot, which was not healing at all, came under the surgeon's knife.

When I had recovered from the surgeon's attack, which certainly made my leg heal quickly, it was decided by Mamma that I should have a bath. This was an excellent idea, as I had not had a bath for three months. Mamma ordered me to get out of bed and follow her to the bathroom. The sentry started to come with me but was given such a 'rocket' by Mamma that he beat a hasty retreat. The bath turned out to be a hot shower, which looked most inviting. Having been shown the shower, I naturally waited for Mamma to withdraw before I stripped, but she showed no signs of moving. I looked rather blank and then took off my watch, which I asked her to hold. She took the watch but still stood her ground. Then I took off my shirt and vest and stood before her in my short pants, quite convinced that she would then withdraw. Not a bit of it! There she stood, and as I made no move, she asked me what I was waiting for. There was nothing for it. The wife of the station-master of Reggio Calabria wished to see me in my birthday suit, so off came my pants and I stood there exposing all my charms to this immense woman. She stood and talked to me the whole time I was under the shower, and when I had finished she held the towel out to dry me! The bath completed, we walked back arm in arm to the ward, certainly knowing each other better than before. I had several baths after this, and Mamma was always present. In the end I got so used to it that I should have felt quite lonely without her.

In mid-February the weather became very warm, so Sister arranged that we should all be allowed to sit out on the terrace for two hours in the afternoon; patients who could not walk were carried down on stretchers. This was a splendid arrangement, as it broke the monotony of our days in the ward and gave us a chance to talk with the other patients from the soldiers' ward. I had been allowed to go to the soldiers' ward to give Daniel his English lessons, but now we were able to do them in the sun on the terrace, from which we had a wonderful view across the Straits of Messina to Sicily. By this time there were several Italian wounded in the hospital, but they lived in a separate ward and sat on the other side of the terrace. Visitors who came to see us on Saturdays and Sundays would walk out on to the terrace and talk with us there. The number of visitors increased every week, and they always gave *us* the attention, completely ignoring the Italian patients on the other side. Most of the visitors were completely pro-British and, despite the bombing, treated us as friends. Their kindness and generosity was quite embarrassing.

At the beginning of March, there was an important *fiesta*, and Sister prophesied that we should have many visitors that day. Her forecast was only too true. They started to arrive at three o'clock, and within an hour the terrace was packed with visitors. It is no exaggeration to say that by four o'clock there must have been a hundred visitors on our terrace. It was a remarkable sight, especially as among our visitors there were several members of the Italian armed forces. A spectator might well have thought that it was a meeting of allies and not enemies. Unfortunately, not one soul went near the Italian patients, who were naturally angry and complained to Musso. He was angry too, and blamed it all on poor Sister. They had a stand-up row, with the result that all visitors were prohibited. This was a bitter blow, as it meant a starvation diet once more.

By this time the fall of Tripoli was imminent, and we scanned the daily newspapers hopefully. In those days Italian propaganda was very amusing. Whenever things were going badly the Italians would 'sink' the entire Mediterranean fleet to fortify their readers for the bad news that would be published two days later. Two days before the newspapers published a report on the fall of Tripoli, all our battleships went to the bottom, and our worthy guard Francesco agreed with us that Tripoli must have fallen. This, of course, proved to be the case.

Shortly after this good news, we were graced by a visit from the Prefect of Reggio Calabria. Before his visit, the hospital was scrubbed and cleaned, Mamma and Musso chasing the unfortunate orderlies from one ward to another. Eventually the stage was set and the great man arrived. No British field marshal at a king's levee could hold a candle to this Fascist official as far as uniform was concerned. Although he was not in the armed forces he was covered in medals, and his uniform of air force blue was richly adorned with gold braid; his cap was of the German type with a large golden eagle above the peak. Musso saluted him about five times a minute, while Mamma and her maidens raised the right arm in good Fascist fashion. He marched into our ward followed by a large retinue, went over to Massué's bed, where he spoke a few words in French, and then marched out again. He neither spoke nor looked at the wicked Englishman and American. A more ridiculous man I have never seen, even in Italy.

Our hospital had its own church attached to the building. A very old priest used to come in from the town to say Mass each Sunday morning. Those of us who would walk were allowed to attend, even if we were not Catholics. I used to go on alternate Sundays, with soldiers from the other ward. The church was filled with the old men and women from upstairs, most of whom had one foot in the grave and whose date with their Maker was close at hand. The poor old things were all lame, deaf or blind and hardly seemed to know what was going on. The old men used to make the most unattractive noises and continually spat on the floor. The women were very quarrelsome, and on one occasion two of them came to blows, eventually being pulled apart by the nuns. Apart from these minor incidents the service was pleasant and the singing quite good. One Sunday the old priest gave a terrific sermon which seemed to cause much excitement among the congregation. Later, I asked Sister what it had been about. Apparently, the priest had said that there were two men who were trying to rule the world, but that God would see that they were defeated. A brave statement to make when people were being arrested in large numbers for anti-Fascist tendencies.

By mid-March, my wounds were at long last practically healed, but before I left I was destined to see some harrowing sights.

At this time the downstairs ward was very full and we were told that any new arrivals would have to come to our ward. A day or two later, two badly wounded English soldiers arrived from Tunisia and were brought into our ward. One of them belonged to the Hampshire Regiment and the other was a corporal in the Durham Light Infantry. The private from the Hampshires had had one leg amputated and the other was broken. The corporal had had an arm amputated and a bad wound in the leg. They had been operated on by the Germans at a temporary hospital outside Tunis and were then flown across to Reggio Calabria. On arrival at our hospital they were taken straight to the operating theatre and their dressings removed. The young soldier from the Hampshires – he was only twenty – was in a ghastly state and we could hear his screams as his dressings were being removed. After being bandaged, they were brought into the ward. Everything went well that night and both patients had a good night's rest. But in the morning the dressings had to be done again, this time in the ward. Mamma warned us that we were going to see something very terrible, and the old doctor asked me specially to take a look at the men's amputations, which he described as a disgrace to any doctor. He started on the Hampshire lad, and as the dressings were being removed the poor fellow's screams of pain were terrible to hear. This was bad enough, but when the dressings were off it was a hundred times worse. The stump looked just as though a dog had gnawed the leg off. The flesh was completely exposed and the roughly sawn-off bone was sticking out from the base of the stump. I have never seen a more ghastly sight. The old doctor told me that in all his long experience he had never seen any amputation so badly done. He told me to ask the boy why it had been done like that, but the lad could not tell us. He had been surrounded by Germans and as he came out of his slit trench a shell from a Tiger tank had hit him. The doctor told me that he would have to do a further amputation when the poor fellow was strong enough to stand the strain.

The same applied to the corporal's arm, which had been sawn off in a similar fashion. The corporal, a Durham miner, was one of the toughest men I have ever met. When his arm was dressed he just bit his lips and never made a sound. The medical orderly in our room – a completely incompetent ass called Antonio – was quite unable to cope with the two newcomers. The result was that when the dressings were removed in the mornings I had to assist by holding the stump of the amputated leg in the air, while Mamma and Anita did the dressings. It was an unpleasant duty, made worse by the agonized screams of the unfortunate patient. The poor fellow seemed to like me doing things for him, and preferred me to move him into different positions rather than let the clumsy Antonio try to do it. This included some very unpleasant daily duties, and I felt that the patient should be moved to a ward where there was a competent orderly. Dominic would have been ideal, but he had left to serve on a hospital train between Russia and Italy. I spoke to Mamma about it and she agreed that the men needed better attention; they were moved the next day to the other ward.

After a day or two the corporal was taken to the theatre to have his arm reamputated. The hospital had no anaesthetic, so the wretched man was only given the so-called local which we had had. The bone was sawn through and the arm properly sewn up, but to do this without anaesthetic was criminal. I saw the corporal the next day and he looked ten years older, although he said his arm was 'champion'. Anita told us that he was the bravest man she had ever seen, as he had not made a sound during the operation, which had lasted an hour and a half. I asked why no proper anaesthetic had been used and was told that the hospital did not possess any. My thoughts naturally turned to the Hampshire man, as the doctor had said he would have to operate again. I felt sure that if they did this operation without anaesthetic, the shock would kill him. I got Sister to get in touch with the *contessa*, who was now head of the Red Cross. At all costs, we had to stop them doing this operation until anaesthetic arrived. The *contessa* was most helpful and promised me that anaesthetic would be obtained for the operation. This was due to take place just before I left, but unfortunately the man got influenza and it had to be postponed. Before going, I got a solemn promise that anaesthetic would be used. I saw the patient before I left. He looked very weak but was extremely cheerful. I have never heard how he got on.

Just before I left the hospital, Dominic came back on leave and visited our ward. He told us that on his last trip from Poland with Italian wounded, there were over four hundred cases of frostbite. No wonder the wretched Italian soldiers surrendered to the Allies in thousands to avoid service in Russia.

Dear old Dominic! He had been a loyal friend. He sung to us that afternoon, accompanying himself on a guitar. He gave us all his address with instructions to come and see him after the war.

On 20 March Musso told me that during the next ten days I would be moved to a permanent camp. Although I had had very kind treatment and charming companions, I was immensely relieved at the prospect of moving.

I waited a week, and then the great day arrived. Sister brought me my battledress, which she had mended, washed and pressed herself. I felt quite strange being in uniform again after three months in hospital. Five others from the downstairs ward were coming with me; we were due to leave the hospital that afternoon to take the train to Naples.

Sister went off to the town in the morning and returned with cakes, wine and cigarettes which she distributed among the six of us. To our grateful thanks she answered once more – 'It is nothing. God will take care.'

The morning was spent in saying goodbye to the various people in the hospital, including the men in the downstairs ward. Then Francesco came into the ward and said that I must go down to the hall, as we were due to leave. I then said goodbye to Walter Grant, Paul Carnes and Jacques Massué. They were a grand trio and had certainly helped to brighten those three dreary months. The date of my departure was 28 March.

As I left the ward, Francesco was standing in the passage with several other Italian soldiers and a lieutenant. I shook Francesco by the hand. He put down his rifle, came smartly to attention and gave me an English salute. I hope he didn't get into trouble for this somewhat un-Fascist display.

My companions for the journey were an odd assortment. One of them, a Scotsman from the Argylls, had flaming red hair; another was a merchant seaman; another a commando with only one arm; the other two were French soldiers, one of whom was weak in the head. I saw the old doctor in the hall and he shook me warmly by the hand. Musso, who was fussing about our escort, gave me the Fascist salute. The escort, which consisted of two *carabinieri* (Italian military police) and four soldiers, had brought a truck in which to take us away, but Musso decided that we should walk. It was his last parting shot and I must admit that it wasn't a bad one. We all took a long and tender farewell of Sister. I had a big lump in my throat when I said goodbye.

We started off towards the town with our escort. As we went down the hill, I looked back and there was Sister standing on the terrace waving her handkerchief. The afternoon was warm and we were soon bathed in perspiration, as none of us had walked more than a few steps in the last three months. We were marched down the main street of the town, much to the interest and amusement of the population – I suppose we were a funny sight – but I must hand it to the German soldiers, who whenever they saw us coming crossed over to the other side of the street and never so much as looked at us.

By the time we reached the police station, we were all completely exhausted. The *carabinieri* gave us benches to sit on and informed us that we should have to wait three hours. This was rather a depressing thought, but we were quite accustomed to sitting about and doing nothing. Our train was due to leave at 7.30 p.m., and at 6.30 we moved from the police station to the railway station. The streets near the station were crammed with German trucks and guns awaiting shipment to Tunis. All this equipment was brand new and must eventually have been left in Tunisia. When we got to the station, we were put in a waiting room reserved for military personnel. I had an amusing conversation with an Italian soldier who spoke excellent English and who had probably been told by the Italian officer to push propaganda on to us. Our conversation went as follows:

'Have you a house of your own?'

'Yes.'

'Have you the key to the front and back doors?'

'Yes, but not on me.'

'Would you like to give those keys to somebody else?'

'It depends on the person.'

'But you might feel uneasy?'

'I suppose so.'

'Well, you see, you English have the keys to our front and back doors – Gibraltar and Suez, and that is why we are in the war.'

'Are you the only country in the Mediterranean?'

'We are the only important one.'

'I'm afraid I disagree, and in any event you cannot have the keys.'

'We shall see. Germany will beat Russia this summer [1943] and then England will be finished.'

'We shall see. Good evening.'

At 7.30 sharp the train came into the station, which was packed with German and Italian soldiers and civilians. The train was already full and it seemed impossible that any more people could get in. Before the train had stopped there was a wild rush of shouting Italians for the doors. Luckily for us, we had two first class compartments reserved, so we did not have to take part in the contest. Eventually everyone was squeezed in and the train moved off. Within five minutes of leaving the station there was an air raid and the train remained at a standstill for half an hour. We then continued on our way, the train stopping nearly every ten minutes throughout the night. We were due to arrive in Naples at six o'clock the following morning but we did not get there until after midday. The journey was uneventful except for one very amusing incident. Two hours before we reached Naples our train halted alongside a goods train carrying oranges and lemons. The temptation was too great for the Italian soldiers on the train. The windows were thrown open and the Italians climbed out onto the goods train. They then proceeded to seize all the fruit they could lay their hands on, which they threw across to their companions in our train. The Italian officer in charge seemed quite powerless to stop them, and after ten minutes the goods train must have been relieved of several thousand oranges and lemons. The *carabinieri* with us also took part in the game, so we had our fair share of the fruit. When the whistle blew there was a frantic scramble to get back through the windows before the train started. It was a most amusing sight and could only have happened in Italy.

When we arrived at the station, the *carabinieri* told us that we were going to a transit camp at Capua some twenty miles north-east of Naples. This entailed changing to another train due to leave at two o'clock. We were marched off to the next platform, where we sat down and waited for the train. As it was a Saturday, the station was very crowded with people going back to the country districts for the weekend, and we were immediately surrounded by a gaping crowd, most of whom seemed highly amused at the Scotsman's red hair. As the hour approached for the train's departure, the crowd became larger and larger. It was soon apparent that there was to be another battle royal for the train. Once again we had reserved seats and did not have to take part in the struggle. The train, a very long one, came in shortly before two o'clock. Half the carriages were cattle trucks with benches fixed inside them. We watched the terrific battle for seats, in which the idea of 'women and children first' did not seem to apply, and then walked quietly to our first class compartment.

The train stopped at every station, and the delays were increased by the pitched battle that took place between those wishing to get out and those wishing to get in. As a result, this journey of twenty miles took just over three hours. We arrived at Capua shortly after five o'clock, very dirty and tired having been travelling for twenty-one hours.

The camp was a mile from the station and just outside the old town, so it did not take us long to reach it. I must admit that my first view of a prisoner of war camp made my morale drop to zero.

The sight of men pacing up and down the wire like caged animals is not very inspiring. We were taken straight to the Italian orderly room, where we handed in our papers and were searched by the Italians. There were two officers who spoke perfect English. One of them, christened 'Daphne' by the prisoners, had sleek black hair, perfectly polished nails and wore large sunglasses. The Italians were extremely polite and did their best to cheer us up. The three English soldiers and the two Frenchmen were taken off to the men's compound, which was separated from the officers' compound by a double wire fence. Daphne then asked me to follow him, and we walked off to a large gateway reinforced with wire. The sentry opened the gate and I walked in. I heard a click behind me. The gate was shut. My life behind the wire had begun.

3

Capua

My arrival in the officers' compound coincided with tea, and all the officers in the compound were in the mess room. Daphne handed me over to the SBO (senior British officer), a New Zealand major by the name of Webb. He in turn handed me over to the adjutant, who then took me to the mess room.

No new boy at school has ever felt more miserable than I at that moment. When I entered the mess room, everyone stopped talking and stared at me as if I were some strange animal. I looked round the room, searching for a friendly face, but all I could see were rows of strange men, mostly unshaven. The adjutant sat me down at a table with three others, who immediately plied me with a hundred questions. A newcomer to a prison camp is usually a very popular person during his first few hours, as he can give the latest 'dope' from the field of battle. As I had been in hospital for three months, I was a dismal failure in this respect, much to the disgust of the people at my table. After a very frugal meal I was taken off to a hut and shown my bed.

The camp was situated on a plain to the north-east of Naples. It was overlooked by a high range of hills to the east, and the now famous Volturno river ran between the hills and the west coast. The officers' compound was very small, being some seventy-five yards long by thirty yards broad. In this small space there were four wooden huts about ninety feet long. Three of these huts acted as sleeping quarters and the remaining one as the mess room. On the north side of the compound were two stone buildings, one a wash-house and latrine, the other a cookhouse. In addition, there was a small wooden hut which was used as a canteen. The little space left over was all we had to exercise in. The whole compound was of course enclosed by a high wire fence, bordered by a road on the south side and by the men's compound on the north. The men's compound was much larger than ours and held over two thousand. There were two other men's compounds further down the road, which between them held a further three thousand prisoners.

I shall not forget my first few days behind the wire. I sank into the deepest depression and walked up and down like an animal in a cage. I had always felt that zoos were cruel institutions, and now I was convinced of it. The other inmates paid no attention to my depression as they had all passed through this stage of 'barbed-wireitis' themselves.

When I arrived at Capua there were twenty beds in each hut. The beds consisted of three wooden boards laid longways between two iron stands. Each bed had a straw mattress, two smelly, dirty blankets, and was as hard as rock. I put my belongings, which consisted of a toothbrush, a razor and some soap, on my bed and walked around to see if I could find anyone I knew. There were only two officers I had ever seen before: Major Simon Ramsay, whom I had occasionally seen in White's Club, and Philip Morris Keating, whom I had often seen at point-to-point meetings at home. They were both extremely kind to me and did their best to make me feel at home. In one of the other huts there were twenty French officers from the Foreign Legion in North Africa. They were a queer collection but really very pleasant. They had all fought in Norway, and had done good work in the Narvik battle.

My life was considerably brightened on the following afternoon by the arrival of Major 'Gussie' Tatham from Caserta hospital. Gussie was also in the Coldstream, but had been attached to the Hampshire battalion in our brigade. This battalion was very badly cut up in the early fighting in North Africa and Gussie was seriously wounded in the arm and stomach. He spent some time in the French hospital in Tunis, where an enthusiastic French doctor cut him about with a knife until the marks on his stomach and arm looked rather like a map of Clapham Junction.

I was delighted to see Gussie again, and we immediately arranged to 'mess' together. This needs some explanation.

At Capua, as in all other camps in Italy, the Italians supplied a certain amount of food, but barely enough to live on. In fact, they were similar to those meals supplied in the hospital at Reggio Calabria. In addition to these rations, each prisoner was given one British Red Cross parcel a week. These parcels contained such luxuries as tinned meat, butter, milk, biscuits, jam, sugar, raisins and prunes and were the beginning and end of a prisoner of war's life. At Capua, the officers formed themselves into syndicates and shared and cooked the contents of their parcels. Gussie and I formed a syndicate of two, drawing one parcel on Mondays and another on Thursdays.

The cooking of the contents of the Red Cross parcels for the evening meal was done on officers' private stoves made from old tins tied together with wire and erected outside the huts. Some officers made the most complicated stoves on which they cooked even more complicated dishes.

Gussie and I soon discovered that we were not very clever at making stoves from old tins. Our first attempts at making a mug from an old butter dish were singularly unsuccessful. The handles were always lopsided, and when we picked the mugs up the handles usually fell off. As soon as we realized that we could not even make a mug, we decided that it was no use even attempting a stove.

We also found the greatest difficulty in manipulating the Italian tin openers, which were unwieldy and blunt. There was only one of these tin openers to each hut, with the result that this odious weapon was constantly in demand.

Gussie was once a very fine athlete and is now no doubt a learned scholar, but he was quite definitely the worst man with a tin opener that I have ever seen. The initial step of piercing a hole in the lid always caused him much trouble; after a struggle, the tin would shoot across the room, coming to rest under a neighbouring bed. I was definitely good at jabbing the initial hole, but there my success ended.

During our gallant struggles with the tin, a dozen officers would be waiting patiently for the tin opener. At first, they were extremely patient, but after a few days they decided that it would be quicker if they opened our tins for us. Naturally, we agreed to this splendid suggestion, as by this time our fingers and thumbs were heavily bandaged.

The same thing happened over the manufacture of our mugs. A very charming and efficient young officer from the Royal Engineers had been watching our pitiful efforts for some days. At last he could bear it no longer, and he volunteered to make us each a mug.

The question of the stove was also very satisfactorily solved. Not having a stove, we used to live on cold meat roll and cold tinned fish, while others were indulging in delicious hot concoctions such as fish pies, jam puddings and pancakes. Our next door neighbours, feeling very sympathetic, told us that we could use their stove in the evenings. This was splendid and the next evening we sallied forth to cook ourselves some fried meat roll and onions. But we had forgotten that making a fire in a small tin stove requires a certain amount of skill. We wasted a box of precious matches, burnt a lot of paper and lay on our stomachs blowing into the stove, but the flames would not play. After half an hour, we supped off cold meat roll flavoured with paper ash. But we were not long in thinking out a solution. We informed our generous friends that we felt that they should use the stove first in the evenings and that we would follow. They seemed delighted with this praiseworthy unselfishness and agreed to the arrangement. Thus, they lit the fire and by the time we took over the stove contained a fiery furnace. One lives and learns in a prison camp. Gussie must have been able to teach his pupils a thing or two outside Classics when he returned to Eton.

The sanitary arrangements at Capua were appalling. When I first arrived in the camp there were about ninety officers in the compound and by the time I left six weeks later there were some hundred and forty. During this period there was only one small washhouse with six cracked basins, and two cement tubs for washing clothes. In the latrines next door only four out of six water closets were in working order. As there were no urinals, these four lavatories were, to say the least, hard pressed. At all hours of the day there was a queue outside the latrines. This disgraceful state of affairs could easily have been rectified by the Italians. The English medical officers and the SBO complained again and again to the Italian commandant, but the answer was always '*Domani*' (tomorrow). Whenever an Italian uses the word *domani*, it may mean anything from tomorrow to next week or next year – in military circles usually the last of these. Towards the end of April, the camp began to get very crowded and the lavatory situation became desperate.

At Capua we had roll call twice a day. At nine in the morning we paraded outside the huts while the *capitano*, assisted by the interpreter, counted us. The evening roll call took place during the Italian tea meal. The *capitano* was quite a good fellow – a schoolmaster in civilian life – and he worried us very little. The interpreter had been a steward on the Rome Express before the war.

During April the weather became increasingly hot, and flies appeared in their millions. If a drop of jam or condensed milk was spilt, it was immediately covered by a mass of flies. Wherever one went the flies seemed to follow, and although an active fly swatting campaign was organized, it did little to improve the situation. Most of us took an afternoon nap, but this was only possible if we were completely covered from head to foot with a sheet. Anyone going into the huts in the early afternoon might well have mistaken the place for a mortuary. The hot weather also encouraged the brown bed bug. This troublesome creature, brown, round and fat, made his abode in the cracks of the bed boards, and it was difficult to dislodge him from his stronghold. All that remained to complete our discomfort were lice, but luckily they never appeared. A hot shower once a fortnight kept the lice away.

On the brighter side, the most enjoyable aspect of Capua was the walks. Each officer was allowed one walk per week, and usually one could manage to get in a second walk in place of someone who did not wish to go. Fifty officers were allowed on each walk, and before setting out it was understood that one gave one's word not to try and escape. An officer on a horse or bicycle and eight guards on foot accompanied us. The walk usually lasted two hours. The relief at getting outside the wire, even for two hours, was immense. It was very cheering to walk through the countryside and villages where life was progressing normally. Sometimes we broke into song while going through the villages, but this was later forbidden. Presumably the Italians did not like us to show high spirits. The country people did not pay a great deal of attention to us, but they gave us the feeling that they were sympathetic. Our walks used to take us over the Volturno river, later to become such a bloody battleground – in fact, all the places we visited on walks were destined to be the scenes of bitter fighting.

One very hot afternoon we were nearing the camp at the end of a walk when we found two German soldiers, lying unconscious and smothered in dust, in the middle of the road. Two English doctors in our party went over to see what had happened to them. It turned out that they had indulged too freely in the local wine. The Italian soldiers, who loathed their German allies, were delighted, as they knew that the matter would be reported and a heavy punishment would be imposed.

The camp entertainments were arranged by a very hard-working officer called Mike Butcher. In addition to arranging concerts and lectures, he got together an excellent choir, which made our Sunday services in the mess room much brighter. Our padre was John Collins. An enormously tall fellow-Etonian, he had stroked the Cambridge eight to victory three times.

Some of the concerts were very good. The *capitano* allowed concert parties from the men's compound to entertain us. These included several professional artists from the London and provincial stages. The music was mostly supplied by the piano accordions which had been presented to British prisoners of war by the Pope.

At least three lectures a week were given in the mess during the afternoons. These lectures covered a variety of subjects, including big game hunting, the whale oil industry, the Boat Race, the Olympic Games, and various military subjects. I was asked to give a lecture on the City, but feared there might be some big financier hidden in the audience who might get up and ask awkward questions, so I refused, but I did agree to give a talk on racing, a subject with which I felt more at home.

A weekly 'brains trust', debates, play readings and whist drives helped to pass the evenings. The French officers were experts at whist, which they took very seriously, groaning with indignation at the incompetence of their English partners.

I took part in one of the debates. The subject down for discussion was 'Who would make the best wife: Marlene Dietrich or Mrs Beeton?' I was given the task of pressing home the claims of the culinary expert, while one of the younger officers supported the glamorous film star. After an amusing discussion, Mrs Beeton won the day. How I should hate to be married to either of them!

A heated and more serious debate took place over the nationalization of industry. Everyone had definite and divergent views on the subject, and the show of hands was awaited with interest. Unfortunately, an air raid interrupted the count and all the lights were turned out. After two hours of hot air and eloquence we never knew the result. I was also made a member of the brains trust. This proved to be a most unhappy choice, as I was quite incapable of answering any question that was put to me – except on one occasion when I was warned beforehand of the nature of the problem.

To many people, the mention of a 'prison camp' immediately conjures up visions of daring escapes and underground tunnels. Several attempts at escape were made at Capua while I was there. All ended in failure, and some in death. I have already given a rough description of the camp, but I should also mention that it was overlooked day and night by sentries on raised platforms, armed with machine-guns and searchlights. The lights around the wire were left on all night, except during air raids, when every light in the camp was turned out. Any officer seen near the wire during an air raid was liable to be shot on sight by the sentries. Escape was no easy matter at Capua, unless the escapee could somehow get smuggled out of the camp during the day. Even then there was the difficulty of money and clothes, and also the fact that the British troops had not then reached Tunis.

Just before I arrived at Capua, an officer had tried to rush the wire during the night. He was riddled with bullets by the guards and killed instantly. Several weeks after my arrival, another attempt ended in tragedy. On this occasion three British parachute troops from the men's compound managed to take part in the Red Cross parcel-drawing fatigue, which entailed a walk with several others to the large shed outside the wire in which the parcels were stored. Here, they managed to hide and change into German uniforms which had been smuggled into the store. The three men got away, but their absence was soon discovered by the Italians. They had two hours' start of an Italian bicycle patrol which was sent out after them. Late that afternoon, they were surrounded in a wood by Italian soldiers and *carabinieri*; realizing that the game was up, they raised their hands in surrender. What happened then has never really been discovered, but the two surviving members of the party swear that the *carabinieri* opened fire on the third parachutist and shot him dead, even though he had his hands in the air. The *carabinieri* hotly denied this and insisted that the man tried to escape. The *carabinieri* at Capua were a very unpleasant group and I am much more inclined to believe the English story. Italian soldiers are very good at shooting their enemies when they are unarmed. Both stories became very exaggerated, and feelings in the camp ran high for several days. The Italians gave the unfortunate victim a military funeral, which was conducted by Padre Collins. As the coffin, in a military wagon, passed the officers' compound, Major Webb called the officers who had lined the wire to attention, and the padre said a few prayers before the procession moved on, escorted by a detachment of British paratroops and some Italian soldiers.

There were two other unsuccessful efforts at escape which happily had no fatal results. Two officers managed to get out of the camp by going on sick parade and getting two other ranks from the men's compound to stand in for them at roll call. The ruse proved successful and they reached Capua station, where they planned to take tickets for the north. Unfortunately, they had celebrated before the event by drinking all the wine in the canteen on the previous night – a foolhardy action that had disastrous effects. While they were at the station one of them, overcome by the effects of the night before, was forced to go to the lavatory. His knowledge of Italian was scanty and he entered the ladies' instead of the gents'. An officer of the *carabinieri*, seeing this strange behaviour, went to investigate, and they were both arrested.

The other attempt was equally amusing, and was even enjoyed by the Italians. One day it was discovered that in the men's compound there was an entrance to a large sewer inside the wire. The top was removed and showed that the sewer was large enough for a man to crawl through. The exit to the sewer was well outside the wire. The news spread like wildfire and everyone wanted to escape. The arrangements got completely out of control, and instead of one or two men going away, about twenty went down the sewer together. The whole escapade was so obvious that the Italians discovered it immediately, and when the twenty slime-covered adventurers made their exit from the sewer, an Italian reception committee was awaiting them! The Italians took it all in good heart. One of the concert parties made up a most amusing song entitled 'Going Down the Sewer', which the Italian commandant enjoyed as much as anyone.

As the end of April approached, more and more prisoners arrived in the camp. The weather got hotter and hotter, conditions became more crowded and the flies multiplied by the million. The battle for Tunis was still raging, but the fall of the city was in sight. The Eighth Army was creeping up from the east and the First Army drawing in from the north. Incoming prisoners assured us that the end was in sight. By the end of the month, conditions had become intolerable. There were now 150 officers in the compound. The central aisles in the huts were full of beds; there were others in the mess room; and the washhouse and latrine situation became impossible. It was essential that a draft to a permanent camp should leave as soon as possible, and the Italians promised every day that this would happen *domani*. Despite the cramped conditions, everyone was very cheerful as the news was so good. I had my first letter from home – one of the most exciting moments in a POW's life.

We saw quite a lot of the Germans, as there was a large German camp on the outskirts of the town. Germans arriving from the Tunisian battlefield were deloused in our baths before proceeding to their camp. One afternoon there was a long queue of Germans waiting outside the baths, energetically scratching themselves. We talked to them over the wire while they were awaiting their turn. They were very annoyed at being lousy and assured us that they had caught the pests from the Italians. They soon harped on the old theme that we should not be fighting one another. One of them remarked that together we could conquer the world. Our spokesman pointed out that we had no wish to conquer the world.

'Of course you don't,' said the German, 'you own three-quarters of it already.' Not a bad reply!

On the evening of 8 May Major Webb announced in the mess room that Tunis had fallen. The news was received with loud cheers, and everyone started to speculate on the next Allied move. Would they come straight on to Italy and release us? Wishful thinking was naturally rampant and we all went to bed in high spirits.

In addition to the good Tunisian news, the Italians brought us other good tidings which affected us personally. The crowding in the compound had become so great that the authorities in Rome had at last ordered that a draft of seventy officers should leave within a week for a permanent camp. Gussie and I immediately put in an application to be included in the draft, and it was with a sigh of relief that we heard, two days later, that our application had met with success. The fly in the ointment as far as I was concerned was that Gussie, Simon Ramsay and another friend of mine, Keith Hillas, being majors, were going to a senior officers' camp, while I was going to another officers' camp. I was very sorry, as we had had amusing times together and Gussie had been acting as my tutor in Italian, a language which I was just beginning to grasp. However, the joy of leaving Capua far outweighed any other snags.

On 11 May, the names of seventy officers were read out and those concerned were warned that they would be leaving at dawn the following morning. We were not told whether we were going to a northern or a southern camp. At that period of the campaign it was an important point, as the southern camps offered better chances of escape when the Allies invaded Italy. We spent the afternoon packing our belongings in cardboard boxes and preparing food for the journey. Mike Butcher arranged a farewell sing-song for later in the evening, but this was cancelled because Gussie had a slight fracas in the Italian quartermaster's office that afternoon.

The great day arrived, and we were roused from our beds at 4 a.m. By 5 a.m. we were all ready, with our parcels firmly tied up with string. The Italians then announced that every officer would be searched by *carabinieri* before leaving the camp, so all the string had to be untied again. The search took a considerable time, but by

6.30 a.m. the party was ready to move. In addition to the draft of seventy officers, there were six hundred other ranks leaving from the men's compound who were also going to permanent or working camps. The train was due to leave at 7.30 a.m. It was a glorious morning, with the kind of blue sky which only Italy can provide. We were all in high spirits and we were certain that our new camp would be an improvement on Capua. Every available Italian soldier in the district had been collected to escort us to the station which was completely surrounded by yet more soldiers. The only train we could see was composed entirely of cattle trucks.

In those days (we soon learned differently) we little dreamed that British officers would be carted around the country like a lot of animals, so we asked the guard where our train was. He pointed to the cattle trucks and mentioned rather dismally that he also had to travel by cattle truck.

Each truck contained three wooden benches which would have made it reasonably comfortable for fifteen officers on a short journey. As it was, thirty-five officers and five guards were jammed into each truck, and the journey took twenty-nine hours.

Once we had piled ourselves into the trucks, we did not have to wait long before the train moved off in a southerly direction towards Naples. We were all delighted to be going south, but we were soon to be disillusioned. The train stopped at Caserta for five minutes and then proceeded north.

We rattled on for hours, some of us sleeping, some eating and others playing cards on the floor. There were no sanitary arrangements of any description on the train – sanitation is a subject which most Italians completely ignore – and anyone wishing to relieve nature had to do so the best way he could, a perilous undertaking with a train tearing along at sixty miles an hour. As the day wore on, the atmosphere became increasingly stuffy, and our old enemies the flies had decided to travel with us. By midday we were covered in dust, very thirsty and extremely bad tempered.

We rattled into Rome at 1.30 p.m., and crowded to the door and windows to look at the Eternal City. I had spent some time in Rome in 1936, when my wife and I had motored down from Florence. On that occasion, when our arrival had been more dignified, we had stayed at the Excelsior Hotel.

Our train drew up in a siding at the main station, which appeared to be undergoing considerable enlargement. The trucks containing the six hundred other ranks and the three majors were shunted onto another train, which left for an unknown destination. Our two trucks remained in the siding for over an hour and were then hitched on to a train making for Florence.

The country between Rome and Florence was uninteresting until we got within twenty miles of the city. The journey from Rome had taken five hours and we crossed the bridge over the river Arno shortly before dusk. The sky was a lovely dark purple, which showed up the city and its surrounding hills to great advantage.

We remained at the station for two hours. Several officers managed to sell their Red Cross soap for considerable sums, good soap being quite unprocurable in Italy. When we left Florence, the sentries told us that our camp was near Bologna, which we would reach about midnight. This proved to be correct as far as timing was concerned, but when we reached Bologna we were once again shunted into a siding, where we spent an uncomfortable night. The train moved on soon after dawn, and at nine-thirty we drew up in the small station of Castelguelfo, just north of Parma, where we were ordered to get out of the train. It was a very dirty and scruffy collection of officers who lined up, blinking in the morning sunshine. The stationmaster and a few civilians regarded us with amusement and, I think, a little sympathy. Four horse-drawn military wagons stood in the station yard, and in these we put our parcels and greatcoats. The tired, unshaven and rather harassed Italian officer who had accompanied us from Capua counted us again and discovered that the only missing members of the party were three Italian guards who had decided to spend the weekend in Rome. The wagons then set off, and we followed on foot along the dusty country lane. The camp was some twenty minutes' walk from the station, and as we approached it speculation about its possible size and amenities was rife. Could it be worse than Capua?

4

Fontanellato

We saw in the distance a tall modern building rising above the trees. It looked much too grand to be a prison camp, but as we got nearer we perceived the familiar sight of khaki washing hanging out of the top windows. It seemed too good to be true. We soon reached the village. At the entrance the name FONTANELLATO was written boldly on a neon sign. A brand new national orphanage rose majestically above the other houses, but the little orphans had never entered their luxurious home – they had been replaced by British prisoners of war.

We swung through the main gateway and came to a halt in front of the steps of our new home. Several faces peered furtively out of the front windows, but hastily withdrew when an Italian officer shouted and waved his arm at them. I thought this rather strange at the time, but was later to learn exactly what it meant.

The stone steps led to an alcove which ran along the front of the building. Several British officers were seated there to take down our particulars. In alphabetical order we were called to a table, where we were asked every conceivable personal detail. This done, we were searched and handed over to the adjutant, who took us inside. Everything seemed very efficiently organized.

The Fontanellato orphanage was a hideous erection, but quite impressive. There were five floors, including the basement and ground floor. In the centre of the building there was a large galleried hall, entered from the front door, which in our time was always kept locked. The hall was originally intended as a chapel for the orphans, and it had an elaborate altar at the north end. This altar was bricked off from the rest of the hall, making a little chapel which was used by the Roman Catholic officers in the camp. The remainder of the hall was used as a writing room, card room, lecture room, theatre and general collecting point for officers. The south end of the gallery was used as a bar. Doors from the ground floor wings led into either side of the hall and gallery. On the ground floor there were four large rooms, two in each wing, with about thirty beds in each. Each wing had its own washrooms and lavatories. The remaining rooms on the ground floor were taken up by the hospital, medical officer's room, orderly room, cigarette and private parcels store, canteen and bank. The floors upstairs were divided into rooms holding thirty, sixteen and six beds, each wing again with its own washrooms and lavatories. The basement contained the quartermaster's stores, showers, baths, kitchens, batmen's dining room and the camp library, which contained a large collection of excellent books.

There is no doubt that Fontanellato was the Ritz hotel of prison camps, and to those of us coming from the filth and stench of Capua, it seemed almost too good to be true.

After I had been searched, the adjutant, Reggie Phillips, an extremely efficient officer, took me to my own room, which was one of the six-bed type. A shave, a wonderful cold shower and a visit to the bank were followed by a drink of vermouth at the bar. As Sophie Tucker used to say, 'the day had started well'.

There were some five hundred officers in the camp and one hundred and twenty batmen. After an excellent cold meal, I decided to look around for anyone I might know, and walked out on to the playing field on the north side of the building. There were two enclosures; the first, a small pebbled courtyard completely surrounded by wire, led into the second, a playing field roughly one hundred yards square, also surrounded by wire with the usual sentry platforms at all four corners.

I soon found several people I knew by sight, but extremely few whom I knew by name. One of the first people I saw was John de Bendern, better known as John de Forest, the one-time amateur golf champion of England. I had known John for many years and was delighted to see him. He is the type of person who can be relied on to brighten any prison camp. I found him the first morning, taking part in one of the strangest pastimes that I have ever seen at a POW camp, namely 'boat racing'. This title is perhaps somewhat misleading, as there were no rivers or lakes attached to the playing field, no rowing boats, skiffs or sailing craft, which one would associate with boat racing. There was, however, a ditch, which ran straight for fifteen yards, then turned sharp left into a drainpipe and emerged again after an underground journey of six feet, continuing on a straight course until it disappeared through the wire. Thanks to the overflow from a spring that had not yet been properly drained by the Italians, the drain contained a constant stream of water, which hurtled along between its narrow banks at a great pace. Here was a ready-made 'Putney to Mortlake'. Boats were made from wine corks. The entrance fee for each race was usually five or ten lire, prize money being given for the winner. The usual field consisted of a dozen boats, the winner pocketing forty lire – not a bad prize with vermouth at six lire a glass!

My first glimpse of John de Bendern was when he was following one of these races. His boat had just become stranded on a sandbank and John was wringing his hands and crying out, 'Is there no justice in this world?' I at once came to the conclusion that all the officers taking part in this sport were completely round the bend. However, within a fortnight I was one of the most enthusiastic of boat owners!

John de Bendern was extremely kind to me, giving me books, cigarettes and any clothing he could spare. He also introduced me to a number of officers whom I knew by sight. These included Dermot Chichester, whose elder brother, Paddy, had been killed on Christmas Eve while serving with our battalion; Dick Black, the well-known amateur rider; Arthur Gilbey, whose family's products most of us have tasted; Dennis Duke, from the Stock Exchange; Delmé Seymour-Evans, Tommy Pitman and several others.

The SBO at the time of my arrival at Fontanellato was Colonel Norman of the East Yorkshire Regiment. He was known in the camp as 'no nonsense Norman'. Soon after I arrived, his place was taken by Colonel Tyndell Biscoe of the Gunners. 'Tindell Biscuit', as he was affectionately known, had arrived from a senior officers' camp at Poppi, together with several other colonels and majors. Colonel Mainwaring, who had been GI to General Montgomery in the desert, also arrived with this party. This was extremely fortunate for us, as he gave a series of interesting lectures covering the period from El Alamein to the advance into Tunisia. I have seldom heard a better lecturer.

The arrival of so many senior officers necessitated a reshuffle of rooms, and I soon found myself in a room for sixteen, instead of six.

Colonel Biscoe was certainly a good sport and he was very popular. His reign as SBO did not last long, and after a few weeks a more senior officer, Colonel de Burgh, arrived at the camp and took over. Colonel de Burgh was a very different person. A strict disciplinarian with a stern expression, he soon decided that the camp needed to be pulled together, and he set about the job without delay.

The Italian staff consisted of a colonel commandant, six other officers, a sergeant-major interpreter and about sixty soldiers. The commandant, Colonel Vicedomini, was a very pleasant person who did everything to make our lives as bright as possible. He could not speak a word of English but was fluent in French. Two of the other officers spoke excellent English; one of them, Camino, had an English mother and wife. Camino was a charming person and, like the commandant, did great work for us after the Armistice. The other English-speaking officer, Prevadini, was a rather tiresome little man.

We were fortunate to have such an agreeable commandant and staff, as I am told that in the early days of the war most Italian prison camp authorities were quite unbearable.

I have already mentioned that inmates were discouraged from looking out of the windows on to the village street. I learned by experience that they were very strict about this. After I had been at Fontanellato a few days, I was having a drink in the bar before lunch. At that moment, two officers who had escaped and been recaptured arrived back with their escort. Natural curiosity prompted me to look out of the window, and I was so absorbed in the proceedings that I failed to notice an Italian officer who was shouting and waving his arms in my direction. I was brought to my senses by the sharp report of a pistol, and two bullets embedded themselves in the wall below the window. In an instant, the few people in the bar were on the floor, and a small procession was led out of the door by John de Bendern on his hands and knees. Despite protests, the Italians were most insistent on this rule, and threatened to shoot to kill on the next occasion. I presume that they did not like the idea of our fraternizing in any way with the civilians who passed up and down the village street.

I had arrived at Fontanellato on 14 May; from then until we left, 9 September, we had four months of glorious sunshine, only occasionally broken by terrific thunderstorms which temporarily laid the dust and cleaned up the countryside. No one could wish for a more perfect climate. We spent most of the day in the open, and seldom wore anything but shorts. Those who could stand the intense heat sunbathed in the courtyard in the afternoon; others took a nap. The bar was open between 11.45 a.m. and 12.30 p.m., and again between 6 p.m. and 9 p.m. Only vermouth was on sale during the morning session, but it was good and quite potent. A peacetime gin and vermouth is a short and sharp drink, but a Fontanellato vermouth was anything up to half a pint, and it was not unusual to drink a pint of vermouth before lunch. The effect was pleasant and soporific. The bar sold Italian red wine in the evening, but this was sadly below the standard of the vermouth. I have never tasted such filthy wine, and no one but a prisoner of war would have dreamed of drinking it. The drink was sold on a ticket system, each officer being issued with one wine and one vermouth ticket per day. There were many abstainers in the camp and their tickets were always in great demand. Wine tickets were also exchanged for cigarettes. When anyone wished to give a party, there was a general round-up of wine tickets by the guests, and the wine was then issued in bulk to the host.

One of the most outstanding personalities in the camp was Bill Rainford, a rear gunner officer from the RAF. A man of energy and imagination, he ran all the sports and entertainments. These included athletic sports, football, football pools, boxing, baseball and concerts. In addition to these activities, Rainford was the originator and head of an organization known as Opportunities Ltd. The functions of Opps were manifold. In a large officers' camp there are many members who wish to exchange articles of clothing, cigarettes, shoes and the like, but who find it difficult to find their opposite number. This difficulty was solved by Opps, who published a weekly list of articles wanted and for sale. In this way the two parties were brought together, and Opps took 5 per cent for their trouble. Opps also employed a number of officers who knew how to sew, and they executed orders for badges of rank, collars and repairs to clothing. Watchmenders, tinsmiths (who made excellent mugs from old tins) and portrait painters were also included on the staff. In fact, if you wanted anything done, you went to Opps. One officer dropped his cigarette lighter down the lavatory, so he went to Opps and they retrieved it. Service indeed!

Rainford's biggest coup was the football pools. Half the exercise field was taken up by a football pitch. It had once boasted some grass, but now had a baked mud surface. Football soon proved popular despite the heat, and Rainford set to work to organize a football league and cup. Each team consisted of seven players, no player being allowed to play for more than one team. In a very short time, there were thirty-five different teams, twenty-two of them entering for the league. The matches lasted fifteen minutes each way. Play took place in the mornings between ten and midday, and in the evenings from four to six. The temperature was nearly always in the eighties, and only 'mad dogs and Englishmen' would have dreamed of playing in such heat.

After starting in quite a small way, football matches became a craze, and even elderly majors and colonels took part in them. The enthusiasm reached its climax when Rainford introduced the football pools, which he ran on similar lines to those held in England. Fourteen matches were advertised for each week, and the forecast coupons had to be handed in on Monday morning. Rainford managed to persuade Prevadini to get the coupon slips printed in Parma, in itself a remarkable achievement. Pool enthusiasts were allowed to fill in as many lines as they wished, each line costing one lira. The lucky winner at the end of the week received anything up to a thousand lire. Interest in the football soon spread among the non-playing members, and the evening matches were watched by three to four hundred people, some sitting in the sun on the touchline and others watching proceedings from the grandstand windows. The crowd gave the players a good deal of barracking, especially in matches at the end of the week, which were crucial to the pools enthusiasts.

Seven a side rugby was also played at Fontanellato, the players being recruited from the very young and from certain other officers who were old enough to know better. The most enthusiastic rugby players were the South African batmen, who I imagine were accustomed to playing under such dangerous conditions.

An excellent sports meeting was also arranged by Rainford, finishing up with an open air boxing competition after dinner. In addition to the sports, some very amusing, and at times exciting, running matches were held during the summer. A chance remark in the bar that one officer could run faster than another would result in a match being arranged. A few extra competitors would be drawn in and the match advertised on the Opps notice board. Two book-making firms immediately sprang into existence, and ante-post betting notices also appeared on the board. The bookies and their touts hovered around the bar waiting to tempt some 'over-vermouthed' officer with fantastic odds on a 'horse' that had no earthly chance of winning!

Exercise was not limited to the playing field – each officer was allowed one walk per week. These started at 8 a.m. and lasted a couple of hours. I enjoyed the walks at Fontanellato more than any other form of recreation. It gave one a great feeling of freedom to get outside the wire, and the countryside was always interesting, specially at that time of the year. The camp was situated in the plain of Lombardy, with the Alps to the north and the foothills of the

Apennines to the south. The Lombardy plain is one of the most fertile in the world, and the Italian farmers certainly make the most of it. Every available inch of ground is under cultivation, and whatever is planted grows with astonishing rapidity and strength. During the war, the majority of agricultural labour was done by women, who worked a good ten hours a day.

The fruits of Lombardy were not confined to the Italians. The messing in the camp was run by a Belgian officer called Blanchard, who managed to get in touch with the agricultural markets, black and otherwise. Thus, in addition to our Red Cross parcels (the contents of which were all pooled) we were able to buy a large variety of fresh vegetables. These, together with the Italian rations of macaroni and bread, gave the messing committee wide scope, of which they took every advantage. There was always enough food, and on the whole it was well cooked.

Those in search of education had ample scope, as there were classes for numerous subjects including foreign languages. Unfortunately, there was no good Italian teacher – a disappointment to me as I had begun to get a smattering of the language at Capua and was anxious to continue with it. I decided instead to study German, which I had learned during my last two years at Eton. It was a strange coincidence that my tutor in this language was another Gussie – this time Captain 'Gussie' Pearce of the Duke of Cornwall's Light Infantry, in civilian life a solicitor. He held a class on two afternoons a week.

Our evenings were spent playing cards and attending lectures or the weekly entertainments provided by the theatrical experts in the camp. Some of these shows were quite good considering the difficulties of clothes and scenery that the producers had to contend with. *Pygmalion*, *The Circle* and *Blithe Spirit* were presented to enthusiastic audiences, the acting in *Blithe Spirit* being exceptionally good. Variety performances were produced once a fortnight by a remarkable officer called Raeder. His Saturday nights – as the revues became known – consisted of a series of turns with Raeder acting as compère.

In addition to these entertainments, Bill Rainford put on a series of 'In Town Tonight'. I featured in the first of this series and talked on London restaurants and theatres. A later series included interviews with Dick Black, who talked on his rides in the Grand National, and Tony Roncoroni, a rugby international, who told us what it felt like to play at Twickenham.

Tony Roncoroni was involved in the only successful attempt to get out of the camp, though he was later recaptured. His method of escape was very ingenious. During the early days at Fontanellato, the surface of the field was so rough that the Italians supplied us during the daytime with spades with which to level it. The escape committee, which organized and approved all tentative escapes, decided that these tools afforded a splendid opportunity. The next thing required was wood; the answer to this was easy, as the batmen's beds were constructed with boards. Under the pretence of levelling the field, a grave was dug, just large enough to hold three people. Bed boards were laid across the top and covered by a thick layer of earth. A narrow entrance to the grave was left open at one end, and was to be filled in when the grave was occupied. Breathing was aided by rubber tubes inserted through the boards and earth.

The following afternoon two officers, shielded by a crowd of people sunbathing, digging or doing nothing in particular, got inside the grave and were buried. At 6 p.m. the field was closed, and the lower sentries withdrawn. By means of juggling with the sick parade return, the absence of the two officers was not discovered on evening roll call and dummies were placed in their beds to deceive the Italian orderly officer on his evening round. Everything went according to plan, and at midnight the two officers rose from the dead and got through the wire at the bottom of the field.

Two nights later, Roncoroni and two others used the same method of escape, everything once again going smoothly. The first two escapees had decided to walk to the Swiss border, some hundred miles away as the crow flies. Roncoroni and his two companions carried forged passes and intended to pose as Spanish workmen boarding the dawn train at Parma, some twelve miles away, when they were to proceed to Como and across the border. The three got out of their coffins at different hours of the night, having arranged a rendezvous outside the camp. Unfortunately for Roncorani, one of his companions missed the rendezvous, mistaking the place in the dark. The other two waited for about an hour and then went off to Parma station. Roncoroni was an enormous man, both in height and in breadth, but definitely had a Spanish look about him. His remaining companion spoke fluent Spanish. Their forged passes were so well drawn up that they had no difficulty at the station; in fact, an officer of the *carabinieri* found them a place in the corridor of a packed train. This was just what they wanted, as nobody took any notice of them, and their plan looked like being a success. But alas, their lost companion lost not only himself but also his head. He had torn his clothes getting through the wire and was in a dishevelled state. However, he went to Parma station, arriving there after the train had left and looking very suspicious. The *carabinieri* immediately pounced on him. When they saw his papers, they immediately remembered the other two 'Spaniards' they had let through an hour earlier. They telephoned Piacenza station further up the line, and told them to stop the train, at the same time giving a description of the prisoners.

It was not easy to mistake Tony Roncoroni, and within a few minutes he and his companion were pulled out of the train and brought back to Fontanellato.

Meanwhile the other two officers had got a good start and all the search parties of the camp authorities had failed to find them. The Italian commandant was naturally perturbed, as if they were not retaken he would probably lose his job. The graves in the field were discovered amid great excitement, and photographs were taken of the scene of the escape. A week elapsed and there was still no sign of the escapees. They had worked out that ten days' walking would see them over the frontier, so we began to have high hopes of their success. However, after being at large twelve days, they were arrested at Como by a frontier guard and brought back to the camp.

The commandant was immensely relieved at their recapture, but he also appreciated that it had been a good effort on the part of the prisoners. All five were sentenced to thirty days in the 'cooler', which did not occasion much hardship.

The only other attempt at escape was the digging of a tunnel underneath a flight of steps leading from the main building. A large number of people took part in the construction of this tunnel, as the displaced earth had to be carried through the dining rooms and taken upstairs, where it was emptied into a disused chimney. Before the tunnel was finished, events in Italy clearly pointed to a possible armistice and Colonel de Burgh gave instructions that it was not to be used except to escape from German intervention. This was a wise decision, as the last thing we wanted was to lose our pro-British commandant. But, the question never arose, as the tunnel was discovered by the Italians before completion.

After these attempts to escape the supervision of the playing field was tightened up and a few extra roll calls were introduced. At night, the Italian orderly officer and a guard visited the bedrooms two or three times, invariably waking everyone by switching on the light and being generally noisy. This was extremely irritating, as it was very difficult to get to sleep because of the constant 'dive-bombing' of hundreds of mosquitoes that clung to the ceiling by day and began their virulent attacks as soon as the lights were turned out.

Before turning to the political and military events which culminated in the Italian Armistice, I must introduce three important members of the Fontanellato community – namely three geese that had been adopted by some officers in the camp. Originally, they were among ten bought from a local farmer soon after they had emerged from their eggs, and I feel sure that, had they known what the future held in store for them they would have wished to return to their shells. The idea was to fatten them up for Christmas or some earlier festivity. Now a gosling is a very delicate creature, and this fact was not sufficiently appreciated by the majority of the camp. Everyone was anxious to see them grow up and grow fat, with the result that the poor creatures were given every conceivable type of nourishment. Within two days of their arrival three of the goslings had died and the remaining seven looked devilish queer. The goose committee then decided that Bemax should be included in their diet, and within two days, their number had dwindled to five. The situation looked serious and Opps Ltd started to advertise as undertakers. A notice was put up asking officers to refrain from feeding the surviving goslings, and for a few days the five showed signs of improvement – so much so, that some bright individual decided it was time they took to water. The unfortunate animals were then launched into the stream and the next day there were only three. This was too much for the owners and the three survivors were removed to a special pen where no one was allowed to touch them. It was a wonderful sight to see the owners marching across the field followed by three waddling goslings, who they encouraged in their promenade by cries of '*Oche, oche*' (Italian for geese). The climax came when the head goose-keeper and his three charges were allowed to go for a walk outside the wire followed by an Italian escort.

The three goslings finally reached maturity and would, no doubt, have made excellent eating had the Armistice not arrived, which necessitated their owners leaving the camp and their geese to the mercy of the German troops, who no doubt appreciated them.

During our time at Fontanellato there were six major events of military and political importance. The military events had, as far as we could see, little effect on the Italian people, but the political upheaval, bringing with it the fall of Mussolini caused intense excitement.

Ever since the fall of Tunis in the early days of May, we had been waiting with growing impatience for the next Allied move, and the bombardment and subsequent capture of Pantelleria on 7 June came as a welcome sign that the invasion of Sicily was not far off. The Italian Press, which had long boasted the impregnability of Pantelleria, soon began to change its tune when it realized that, for the first time in military history, a fortified position was about to be forced into submission by air and naval bombardment alone. The capture of this small but important base no doubt gave the Italians a taste of what was coming to them when more important objectives were at stake. From that moment, I think both the Italian military and the civilian population recognized that the game was up.

At 3 p.m. on 9 July we were awakened from our afternoon siesta by someone shouting out of the window that the invasion of Sicily had begun. In a moment, the sleeping camp sprang to life and possibilities of a quick collapse in Sicily were eagerly discussed. Colonel Mainwaring, who knew the methods of General Montgomery better than anyone, prophesied that the campaign would last about six weeks, which proved to be a remarkably accurate forecast. The Italians received the news with the utmost calm. There is little doubt that many of them even regarded the event with satisfaction, as it brought the inevitable end nearer still. The Sicilian campaign went as smoothly as the most optimistic of soldiers could have wished.

During the next few weeks rumour, an animal that flourishes in a prison camp, ran riot. Each day produced a bigger and better story until it was impossible to believe anything one heard. It was, therefore, hardly surprising that when the biggest Italian bombshell of the war – the fall of Mussolini – was announced on 25 July, quite a number of people refused to believe it.

That morning, I had gone to take a shower before breakfast, and while soaping myself under a jet of delightfully cold water I was informed by my neighbour that 'Mussolini has been kicked out and a bloke called Bolio, or something like that, has taken over'. I received this important announcement in silence, thinking it yet another rumour. On the way back to my room, I was hailed by several very excited officers who repeated the story and who also informed me that the 'other bloke's' name was Badoglio. I then began to think that it might be true. When I reached my room, I looked out of the window and saw the commandant haranguing the Italian soldiery, who seemed very excited and extremely pleased with life. In the guard room opposite our window hung the usual picture of Mussolini. After the commandant's address, an Italian sergeant entered the guard room, hurled Mussolini's portrait on to the floor and solemnly swept the remains out of the door. The passing civilians seemed equally exalted by the news. The end of Fascism meant the end of many injustices. Above all, it seemed that the end of the war was very near, as far as Italy was concerned.

The Italian newspapers always arrived in the camp about eleven o'clock and were sold in the canteen. A news service run by Larry Alan of the Associated Press and later by Raeder dissected the news and stuck up the salient points on a special board in the main hall. The papers on 25 July were most interesting. The fall of Mussolini was announced in enormous type. Fascism was abolished by law, Badoglio was a fairy prince and everything was going to be happy ever after. Within a few hours, Italian enthusiasm had a cold douche. In a broadcast, the new Italian leader announced that the war would continue as before. It was fairly obvious that Badoglio was playing for time – Rome was not built in a day and twenty years of Fascism could not be uprooted overnight. In addition, there were considerable numbers of German troops in the country.

During the next few days, there was a considerable change in the attitude of the Italian Press toward the British and the Americans. The latter were no longer referred to as the 'gangsters of the air', and the startling stories of British murder and pillage in Sicily disappeared. The camp news service did not waste words over the fall of Mussolini. A large poster appeared in the hall on which were printed only two words – *Benito finito*.

In the nearby town of Parma, the news was received with the greatest enthusiasm, and an effigy of Italy's fallen hero was dragged through the streets. In the original Fascist conquest, Parma had been the last of the Italian towns to give way, and since that date the province of Parma had contained an anti-Fascist majority.

As far as we were concerned, the change of government brought little alteration. Behind the wire, nothing ever changes. One important thing for us was the speed-up in the receipt of mail. There is little doubt that Badoglio's government practically did away with the censorship of our letters. Most of them arrived unopened, and, just before the Armistice, letters were arriving from England within ten days of their despatch.

By 10 August it was apparent that the end of the Sicilian campaign was in sight, and on 17 August the Italians announced the fall of the island. Once again, this military defeat was received with complete calm by the Italians. I could not help thinking what the English reaction would be if the enemy occupied the Isle of Wight!

We celebrated the fall of Sicily with a Sicilian dinner. Our mess president, Blanchard, produced an excellent seven-course meal and began searching his brains and his larder for an even better and bigger dinner for us to have on Armistice night.

The period between the fall of Sicily on 17 August and the Allied invasion of the mainland on 3 September seemed to drag more than any other. So near and yet so far. Some people thought that the Armistice negotiations were in progress and that the Italians would give up the struggle before our invasion of the mainland. My thoughts went back to the hospital at Reggio Calabria. What I would have given to have been there still!

The fourth anniversary of the outbreak of war brought the welcome news that British forces had landed practically unopposed at Reggio Calabria and at other places along the southern tip of Italy. Excitement was intense and rumour knew no bounds. In an effort to give us a moderately accurate picture of the situation, our camp intelligence staff issued a daily 'sitrep' (military term for situation report). A good deal of its content came from the BBC, which some of the Italians listened to and then unofficially passed on to us. The sitreps, rightly or wrongly, were very optimistic and the end of our captivity seemed near.

It is easy to be wise after the event, but I was always convinced that the Germans would not allow the Italians to give up some eighty thousand British POWs, the large majority of whom the Germans themselves had captured. I felt certain that the Germans would try to move us as soon as possible, and the presence of German troops in the district increased this gloomy foreboding. But by 1 September almost all the Germans had left the village and had moved towards Parma. I remember writing a letter to my mother, warning her that there might be a snag to our return. Fearing that the censor might object if I mentioned that there were Germans in the district, I wrote that we were fortunate to have so many chamber pots in the camp. I hope she understood!

Some ten days before the Armistice, a formation of seventy-five

Flying Fortresses flew over the camp. We noticed that one of the planes was in difficulties; smoke was pouring from its engines and it was gradually losing height. Then a white speck appeared in the sky – one of the crew had baled out. The parachutist made a leisurely descent, and it looked at one moment as if he would land conveniently in the prisoners' playground! He did not reach the camp, but came down in a field about two miles away. There was great excitement among the Italian soldiery. A light tank of very antique vintage roared off down the village street, followed by a platoon of Italian infantry, armed to the teeth and travelling in a truck. A tank and a platoon of Italian infantry stood quite a good chance against an unarmed, and probably injured, American airman. Meanwhile, the plane came lower and lower, and shortly after passing over the building banked steeply and disappeared behind some trees. A column of black smoke rose into the sky – the plane had crashed, killing the remainder of the crew. The truck and tank returned victorious. The Italian soldiers proudly displayed the parachute and then lifted the injured American airman from the back of the truck. After examination by the Italian doctor, it was discovered that the American had broken his toe. The Italian Army had gained a glorious victory at last.

The first week in September found us all on tenterhooks. Sitreps appeared throughout the day. The end was in sight. Those who had wagered that we would be home by Christmas started to calculate their winnings. But to many of us, the recollection of the German troops in the district had a sobering effect.

At eight in the evening of 8 September, the bar had its usual crowd of clients. Spirits were high. Suddenly, there was a great commotion outside. Boys and girls were tearing down the street on bicycles shouting '*Pace! Pace!*' An Italian sergeant was standing on his head in the courtyard – strange behaviour even for an Italian sergeant – and others were dancing and embracing each other.

The great moment had arrived at last. Badoglio had asked for an armistice. In a second, the building was in an uproar. The school was to break up at last and the boys were naturally very excited. Old lags, who had spent the last three years lying on their beds smoking cigarettes, growing beards, and reading pornographic literature, hoisted themselves up and waddled down the passage to see what it was all about.

Yes – it was a great moment while it lasted, especially for the sitreps service, which proceeded to announce landings of British troops in every conceivable place except Rome. But what was wanted was a cool head and steady nerves, and, by the grace of God, we had these in the person of Colonel de Burgh, the SBO.

Immediately he heard the news, Colonel de Burgh held a conference with the Italian commandant, and then ordered all the officers and ORs to assemble in the main hall. The noise was worse than the parrot house in a zoo. There was little room to move and precious little air to breathe. Colonel de Burgh mounted the rostrum and there was an immediate hush. I shall never forget the tense atmosphere as we waited to hear what the SBO had to say. One could have heard a pin drop. Colonel de Burgh never wasted words and he made no exception on this occasion.

'Gentlemen', he said, 'I have been informed by the Italian commandant that the Italian government has asked for an armistice. Beyond that I know nothing, but the commandant has promised to keep me in immediate touch with the situation. In the meantime, it is absolutely essential that everyone keeps perfectly calm and behaves like a British officer. No one is to look out of the windows or make demonstrations of any kind with the civilians. No one is allowed outside the building. Everyone will parade in the courtyard at 9 tomorrow morning, when I will give you further details of the situation.'

That was that. No fireworks, but plain common sense. The more stolid members of the community continued their games of bridge, others continued to drink their wine, and the rest went off to bed. I don't think many people slept that night. The mosquitoes, no doubt unaware of the Armistice, continued their incessant attacks.

Everyone was up in good time the next morning. By five minutes to nine we were on parade. At nine o'clock sharp the SBO appeared on the steps, and once again everyone stopped talking. I cannot remember Colonel de Burgh's exact words, but the gist of his remarks was as follows.

War Office instructions to prisoner of war camps were to stay put. The Italian commandant had definite information that fighting was going on between German and Italian soldiers. The commandant considered it very probable that the Germans would arrive to take over Fontanellato, in which case he was going to defend the village with the force under his command. The SBO had considered offering our services to the commandant to help him defend Fontanellato, but had decided that he did not wish to do anything which might embarrass our own Government. He had, therefore, decided to evacuate the camp to some nearby locale, should the necessity arise. If the commandant had information that the Germans were approaching the village, the alarm would be blown, whereupon everyone was to fall in by companies on the playing field. The wire had been cut at the bottom end of the field, giving us a quick line of withdrawal. Everyone was to pack in his kitbag what he considered necessary for a two- or three-day sojourn in the countryside and to draw a certain amount of food from the quartermaster. Greatcoats and blankets would not be carried. The SBO did not know how long we should have to live out – perhaps we would not have to leave the camp at all – but he did not think that it would be for more than four days. Immediately the parade was over, officers were to go and pack their belongings and be prepared to move at a few minutes' notice. In the meantime, Colonel Mainwaring was to go out with Camino and reconnoitre a suitable lying-up place.

Short, concise and to the point. It was not going to be so easy after all.

We all hurried off parade and gathered together our belongings. It was difficult for those people who had a lot of kit to know what to take. It was easy for me, as I only had the clothes I stood in and a toothbrush. There was a considerable supply of cigarettes and tobacco in the private parcels store, and the lucky owners stuffed their kitbags with what they could carry and also gave a lot away to their friends.

For the next hour we all sat on our beds waiting for the alarm, but nothing happened. The sitrep services announced landings at La Spezia, Livorno, Trieste and Genoa, but where this information came from I don't know. It may have come from the Italians, but I cannot believe that it came from the BBC, as it was alleged to have done. Whatever its source, it led us to believe that the situation would soon be completely under control and that the Germans would be forced to leave the country. Had we not had this completely erroneous information, the majority of us would have adopted very different tactics during the next few days, and many more of us would have succeeded in reaching our own lines.

Everything remained quiet and, at eleven oclock, the bar opened in the usual manner and Blanchard prepared an excellent lunch of cold salmon and new potatoes. We began to think that the scare was over and that the Germans, faced with these numerous landings, were hastily withdrawing from the country.

I must frankly admit that I was relieved that Colonel de Burgh had not offered our services to defend Fontanellato. The Italian commandant was a very brave man, but the soldiers under his command hardly inspired one with confidence. We should most certainly have ended up defending Fontanellato by ourselves.

Just when we were preparing to go down to lunch, the alarm was blown. There was a general rush to leave the building and the cold salmon. In an incredibly short space of time, the companies were lined up on the playing field ready to move off.

The last view that I had of the defenders of Fontanellato was three soldiers being pushed into a slit trench by a terrified Italian officer, and another six taking refuge in the pigsties, much to the surprise and disgust of the inmates. The commandant, who remained at his post, was taken prisoner by the Germans and later removed to Poland. He was a very gallant gentleman.

The camp had been divided into four companies plus a head-quarters company, which consisted of Colonel de Burgh's staff and the other ranks. Each company had been given a certain amount of Italian money, provided by the commandant from his own pocket.

Within a few minutes of forming up the companies marched through the wire, led by Colonel Mainwaring and Camino. One officer, who had sprained his ankle, rode a horse supplied by the Italians. As we walked through the gap in the wire, Ronnie Noble, an official war photographer who had been captured at Tobruk, took some pictures with a camera borrowed from the Italians.

We were all in battle dress, a stifling attire for a summer's day in Italy, and as we trudged across the fields the perspiration poured down our faces. Little groups of Italian peasants came out to watch us as we passed their farmhouses, and at any halt they willingly supplied us with drinking water. A German Junkers 52 appeared on the horizon, flying very low, and we immediately scattered in all directions, throwing ourselves on the ground to avoid detection. However, as most of us still wore the large red patches on our backs which denoted a prisoner of war in Italy, the occupants of the plane could hardly have failed to see us.

We walked on for nearly two hours, and finally reached the position that Colonel Mainwaring had selected. This was a small wood surrounded by a high grass bank and open stubble fields bordered by vines. The various companies were scattered under the vines, with headquarters company taking up a position in the wood. We were told that we should remain there until nightfall. Most of us took off our shirts, which were soaked with perspiration, and laid them out in the sun to dry. The first stage of our move had been accomplished without a hitch.

Before continuing the story, I would like to pause for a moment to consider some 'might-have-beens'.

I have already mentioned that the War Office instructions were to 'stay put'. Many SBOs of prison camps in Italy followed these instructions to the letter, with the result that their camps were taken over by the Germans. The most extraordinary example of this unimaginative behaviour was at Chieti, in the south of Italy, where some two thousand officers were forced, under threat of court martial, to remain inside the camp for several days, until the Germans arrived and took them to Germany. Chieti was only about fifty miles from British troops, and, had the inhabitants of the camp been allowed to disperse, at least ninety per cent of them would have got home. A few officers, disregarding the threats of court martial, escaped from their English guards and reached home safely.

Had Colonel de Burgh behaved in the same unimaginative manner, we should have suffered a similar fate and would have missed our three months' vacation in Italy. As it was, Colonel de Burgh quickly realized that the situation had changed for the worse, and made an entirely fresh appreciation. He stayed put in the district, but took the precaution of moving us out of the camp. If the situation improved, all we had to do was to return to the camp, and if it deteriorated further we were in a position to disperse. His decision proved one hundred per cent correct, and those officers who were lucky enough to get home have Colonel de Burgh to thank for their good fortune.

Two hours after we had evacuated Fontanellato, two German tanks and a company of infantry arrived to take over the camp. The Italian soldiers ran away, leaving the commandant to face the music. The Germans were furious at finding the building empty and gave vent to their feelings in a strange manner. They entered the building, drank all the wine they could lay their hands on, ate our cold lunch and then methodically smashed everything in the building. The doors and cupboards were smashed with rifle butts; books, letters and papers were torn up and hurled, together with our clothes, out of the windows. They then loaded as many cigarettes and Red Cross parcels as possible on to their trucks and sold the remainder, together with our clothes, to the civilian population. Officers who later returned to the camp to collect belongings after the Germans had gone reported an amazing spectacle of disorder.

Let us now return to the late inmates of the Fontanellato orphanage, who are still resting under the vines and eating more grapes than are good for them.

During the afternoon several Italian soldiers passed by, all carrying their suitcases. They were the advance guard of the mass desertion that took place in the Italian Army as soon as the Armistice was signed. They informed us that they were returning to their homes and that severe fighting was taking place in Parma. In actual fact, the garrison at Parma did show a little spirit, but this soon subsided when a few German tanks appeared on the scene.

When darkness arrived, the SBO gave the order to move to a position further away from Fontanellato and one that afforded more cover. We crept quietly over the fields and finally reached a ravine, through which ran a small stream with wooded banks on either side. An adjacent field of maize provided us with excellent cover. The companies were split up along the banks and in the maize field, the SBO and his staff taking up their position in the wood.

It was a very hot night and the mosquitoes were as merciless as ever. Very few of us slept more than a few hours. We listened all night to the roar of traffic on the main Parma–Milan highway, and also to the electric trains that passed on the nearby railway at regular intervals. The road traffic was continuous and it sounded as if an armoured division was moving north. Shortly before dawn, an ammunition dump at Parma was set on fire and we could hear the popping of the small arms bullets as they exploded. Then a plane flew very low over our position and dropped a flare, lighting up the surrounding countryside.

The blowing up of the ammunition at Parma, the noise of the traffic moving north and the constant stream of trains during the night made us more convinced than ever that the Germans were evacuating the country while the going was good. We still believed in the landings at La Spezia, Genoa and Trieste, and the next morning these landings were again confirmed by our intelligence staff.

The next day was, I think, the longest I have ever spent. We kept under cover all the time, knowing that the Germans were in the district and expecting them to find us at any moment. The Italian community was most helpful. Several Red Cross parcels were procured for us from the camp, and these were divided up among us. Camino and Prevadini had changed into civilian clothes and they toured the surrounding district in an attempt to find out more definite information. They also obtained more civilian clothes, most of which were handed over to members of the sitrep service in order that they also could wander about in search of further news.

Colonel de Burgh realized by midday that it was most improbable that we would ever be able to return to the camp, and that the problem of feeding six hundred men would soon become insoluble.

By five o'clock that evening, with the help of Camino and Prevadini, no less than two hundred officers and men had been taken in by local farmers and most of them supplied with civilian clothes. The local girls were most helpful and seemed to be enjoying the situation thoroughly. In one case, three of them arrived at our hideout with an Italian man and two sets of civilian clothes. Two officers changed into the clothes and then walked back in daylight arm-in-arm with a girl apiece, as if returning from an afternoon's stroll. All the Italians in the district must have known where we were, and it says a lot for their loyalty to us that no one betrayed us to the Germans.

During the afternoon it was arranged that those who had not been billeted with Italians should move off to the mountains, two companies to go that night and the remainder the following night. We were to move in companies until we had crossed the Via Emilia, the famous road running between Parma and Milan. Once safely over the road, we were to split up into twos and threes and fend for ourselves. The plan was to hide up in the Apennines until the Allies had completed the job – probably a matter of about ten days. We were all, I think, immensely relieved to be going, as the strain of hiding so close to the Germans was beginning to tell. Luckily, the company to which I belonged was scheduled to move that night as soon as it was dark.

Before our departure we had one disturbing scare. At six o'clock we were sitting in the bushes smoking cigarettes and discussing plans when a terrified Italian sergeant arrived and told us that the *tedeschi* (Germans) were coming. It looked as though the game was up. However, it proved to be a false alarm. A platoon of German infantry had passed down the road but, little suspecting that six hundred English soldiers were just around the corner, they continued on their way.

We were already divided up into platoons and sections, but it remained to decide who would go with whom when it came to splitting up. Our section was commanded by Ronald Orr-Ewing of the Scots Guards, and it was decided that when we divided he and I should go together. The platoon commander was Major Donald Nott, DSO, MC, of the Worcestershire Regiment. We were fortunate in having Donald Nott, as in addition to being a very capable officer he was one of the few people who possessed a good compass.

After what seemed like an eternity, darkness descended and we were given the order to move. Colonel de Burgh saw us just before we left and wished us all good luck. We were in good spirits, as shortly before leaving we were informed by a member of the sitrep service, who had been touring the countryside on a bicycle, that he himself had heard on the wireless that British troops had landed in France in the neighbourhood of Boulogne. These were the last words we heard from the famous sitrep service – it had kept up a high standard to the last!

Our company numbered just over one hundred officers, divided into three platoons and a company HQ. We moved off into the night. Although everyone did their best to move quietly, it was impossible to move a hundred men without making a certain amount of noise. We had two objectives to make before we could split up. The first was the railway and the second the Via Emilia. They lay within four hundred yards of each other and were between four and five miles from our starting point.

Colonel Burn, the company commander, and Major Nott walked at the head of the procession, which wound its way stealthily through vineyards, fields of clover and stubble. For the first hour our progress resembled that of a carrier pigeon when first released, going round in a large circle before finally hitting the trail. It was a very warm night and we were soon bathed in perspiration. Judging from the traffic we had heard on the previous night, it was going to be no easy job to cross the road and railway. But fortune was on our side, as on this particular night there was no traffic on the road and the trains seemed to have stopped to allow us to cross.

We had one nerve-racking moment when we were executing our preliminary circle. Donald Nott had lost his bearings and we came to a halt on a road. At any moment we expected German transport to appear or a patrol to surround us. To make matters worse, all the dogs in the neighbourhood started to bark. Colonel Burn went to a nearby house to ask the way, and in a few minutes we were retracing our steps through the fields. After completing a semicircle, we hit on the stream we had been searching for, and from then on nothing could stop us. As we passed the farmhouses with their high granaries, dogs barked and an occasional head would pop out of a window. The moon had risen, turning night into day. Panting and sweating, we crept along in the shadow of the vines and hedges, hoping every moment to see the railway before us. After travelling in this manner for three hours, we came to a halt alongside a farm which specialized in the growing of melons, the majority of which, unfortunately, were unripe. We sat down while Donald Nott made a reconnaissance. The melons, though unripe, made useful pillows as we lay on our backs staring into the starlit heavens.

Donald Nott soon returned with the news that the railway was a few hundred yards ahead of us, and beyond the railway was the Via Emilia. Two more fences to negotiate and then *sauve qui peut*.

We approached the railway by platoons, with our platoon in the lead. It constituted quite a formidable obstacle, as there was a small but steep embankment leading up to it, and parallel with the lines were four strands of signal wires about a foot off the ground. The latter were very difficult to see, even in the bright moonlight, but if they were touched the noise would echo along the line and eventually reach the signal box a quarter of a mile down the line to our left. Fidenza station was some distance away to the right. One by one we crawled up the embankment, and one by one we hit those wretched signal wires, causing a loud 'twang' to echo the whole way up the line. I shall never forget those wires – we tried so hard to avoid them but most of us failed. I thought there might be a German sentry in the signal box, who, seeing us crossing the line, would open up with a machine-gun.

The wires twanged louder and louder, but nothing happened and no train arrived to mar our progress. We were all soon over, reformed, and advanced towards the final obstacle, the Via Emilia, which showed up like a white ribbon in the moonlight. This road, which the previous night had thundered with the passing of German vehicles and tanks, now lay quiet and inviting.

The Via Emilia, like the majority of Italian *autostrade*, was bounded on either side by a high wire fence. When the order to cross the road and disperse was given, this double fence reared its ugly head as if reminding us that this was the ancient Via Emilia and not just an ordinary road.

The charge that followed the order to disperse would have made Balaclava look like a donkey race. A running jump and onto the wire fence. Those officers of smaller stature who missed the mark retired a few paces for a second attempt. Others just made the height and lay suspended across the top wire, lashing out furiously with their legs in order to propel themselves to the other side. This process was repeated on the other side of the road. By the time the whole company was across, the wire fence lay flat on the ground as if a regiment of tanks had just passed over it.

Once safely across, we looked round for our partners, like a pack of hounds checked on the plough. Then, having joined up, we disappeared by twos and threes into the night.

The first stage of the great trek south had begun.

5

Seven wasted weeks

I soon found Ronald Orr-Ewing after the mad scramble over the road, and we walked off across the fields in a southerly direction. It was remarkable how quickly the company had sorted itself out; after walking for only a few minutes we seemed to be quite alone. The going was fairly easy to begin with, mostly over flat stubble or clover fields, but as we approached the foothills of the Apennines we both began to feel the strain. It had been our original intention to keep walking all through the night, but we were not as fit as we imagined. An occasional game of football does not build one up for a long tramp. The longer we walked the more thirsty we became. We tried picking bunches of grapes and squeezing them into our tin mugs, but this did not even begin to quench our thirst. It was past midnight and was therefore too late to ask for water at a house, so we decided to keep going until 2 a.m. and then spend the night in some place where there was adequate cover. We plodded on in silence for another two hours, and then, having climbed a steep hill, we decided to sleep under some vines quite close to a small wood into which we could withdraw at daybreak.

We were both dead beat, but sleep seemed impossible unless we could get something to drink. There was a small farm a few hundred yards away, but we did not like to wake the owners at that hour of the night. Just when we were despairing of ever sleeping or drinking, fortune gave us a remarkably lucky break. We heard the unmistakable noise of a bucket being lowered into a well. It seemed too good to be true. Who could be drawing water at this hour? We looked around and soon saw, halfway between us and the farm, a man standing by a well. He had his back to us and as we advanced towards him in the moonlight he did not hear us. We came right up behind him and then wished him good evening. He immediately dropped the bucket and whipped round as if he had been stabbed. It was obvious that he was extremely frightened. When he had recovered, he started to talk at a furious pace. When we could get a word in, we informed him that we were escaped English prisoners and that we wanted a glass of water. His relief was immense and he told us to help ourselves. The icy cold water from the well was most refreshing, and the Italian looked on in astonishment as we emptied mug after mug. He explained to us that he was a soldier. When the English landed he had been stationed at Reggio Calabria; he had immediately deserted from his regiment and had made his way home by train. When he first saw us he thought we were Germans, which accounted for his agitation. We bade him good night and arranged to meet him at the well in the morning.

Our thirst satisfied, we threw ourselves down under the vines and went to sleep. At dawn it became rather cold, so we got up and moved into the wood, where we remained until 8 a.m. As we were leaving, I caught my foot in some brambles and fell flat on my face, letting out a string of oaths as I went over. A voice from behind a nearby bush exclaimed, 'That must be an English officer'. We looked around and saw three officers from Fontanellato. They had reached the wood while we were asleep and were planning to stay there until the next night. We spoke to them for a few minutes and then went off to the well. I next saw them four months later, in a prison camp in Czechoslovakia.

Our friend from the previous night kept his appointment at the well and talked to us while we waited. He told us that there was a woman living in the next farmhouse who spoke good English and who he was sure would help us. A small boy was immediately despatched to the farm to find out if we could go there, and soon returned with the answer that the woman would be delighted to see us.

If we had gone to sleep thirsty and had never seen the man at the well, and if we had never met the English-speaking woman, it is possible that we would have got back to England. We would have continued to walk south rather than wasting the seven precious weeks that I will describe in this chapter. It was a costly drink, however satisfying. But it is no good looking backwards. Fate would no doubt have arranged for us to meet other people, who would have played a similar part in our story.

The little boy led us off to the farmhouse where we saw a woman standing outside the door nursing a small baby. She was of the peasant, or, as they are known in Italy, *contadino* class. She wore a black dress with the usual handkerchief tied round her head. Lucia welcomed us warmly. She was a trifle shy but spoke excellent English. Her husband was in the Army but was a prisoner in Canada, and she lived in the farmhouse with her two children and father-in-law, a doddery old man of seventy-five. Lucia was quite young and pretty, but was beginning to show signs of the hard work that all women of her class in Italy are subject to – when they are not having babies. No one could have been kinder or more helpful to us than Lucia.

She gave us a splendid breakfast and then warmed up some water for us to shave with. Then we sat in the sun for the rest of the morning, discussing what our next move should be.

Lucia's farm was two miles from the town of Fidenza, which we could see in the distance. The farm was some way from the road, and although there were Germans in the town Lucia assured us that they would not come that way. It had been our intention to move on again that night, but Lucia insisted that we stay the night with her. She said that she was frightened of Fascists and Germans, but that if we stayed she would feel much happier. I found it difficult to understand what we could have done for her if Fascists or Germans had arrived, and we pointed out to her that she ran a risk in having us there. She said that she did not mind that.

We agreed to stay the night in the barn. Lucia killed a chicken which she gave us for dinner with fried potatoes, smoked ham and wine. The old father-in-law, Anna and the baby all sat down to dinner with us. The baby, who was eight months old, had an astonishing diet and an equally astonishing appetite. It began its dinner by feeding from its mother's breast, a slightly embarrassing habit, but one which we soon got accustomed to in Italy. After a short interval, the baby then turned its attention to a glass of cow's milk, which would have satisfied a child of similar age in England, but in a few minutes it was screaming for more. Lucia then gave it a slice of smoked ham, which was devoured with relish. To finish off this square meal, the child knocked back a glass of wine and then went to sleep on its mother's lap.

The next day, Ronald and I tried to find out more news of what was going on. Richard Brooke (Scots Guards) and Jack Younger (Coldstream), who were stopping in a nearby house, came over to see us. They were as much in the dark as we were, so we all decided to go into the hills, find a house with a radio and await the arrival of our troops. We were still under the delusion that landings had taken place at La Spezia and Genoa.

Lucia informed us that she had a brother who lived near Bardi, a small town in the hills some twenty miles from Fidenza. Her brother, who had married an American, spoke English and also had a radio. This seemed to be the answer to our prayer. Lucia assured us that her brother would be delighted to see us and that he would be able to help us. She implored us, however, to stay one more night with her, and this we agreed to do, arranging to leave for Bardi the following night.

Lucia's brother, Giuseppe Dotti, had a house in the small mountain village of Monastero Gravago, three miles south of Bardi. We reckoned that it would take us about two days to walk there across country. Richard Brooke and Jack Younger arranged to stay on a few days at their present lodgings.

We spent the next day resting, and also attempting to be of some assistance to our hostess. But Lucia refused to allow us to do any work. She had a cow, some chickens, a pig and a sheep which she attended to herself, while the old man looked after the children. We asked if we could buy some eggs from her to take on our journey, but she answered that she would not sell eggs to prisoners of war. She insisted on giving them to us free of charge, despite the fact that at that time eggs were fetching fabulous prices.

We had a farewell dinner with Lucia, and after she had supplied us with a map and shown us the best route we marched off into the night. I shall never forget Lucia's kindness to us. She was the first *contadino* we had met and her generosity gave us every confidence for the future.

We soon reached a secondary road, which we followed for a short distance before branching off across country. At that time, we were still very conscious of Germans and Fascists, expecting the roads to be full of enemies who would be searching for us in cars or on bicycles. In fact this was far from being the case. The Germans were too busy consolidating their positions in Italy to worry about English prisoners, and the disrupted Fascists had not had time to get together again.

If we had only known the exact situation, and if we had not been misled regarding the Allied landings, I think that the majority of us would have got home. All we had to do was to obtain some civilian clothes, go to a railway station by night and take a train to Naples, where we could have awaited the arrival of our own troops. The trains were packed and there was no German or Italian supervision of passengers. During the first three days after the Armistice, trains actually ran down as far as Bari in the south of Italy. The only person I know who boarded a train as soon as possible was Colonel

Mainwaring, who did go down to Naples and stayed there until our troops arrived.

As it was, with the information given us the majority of us walked off into the mountains, expecting to wait there for about ten days and then join up with the British troops at either La Spezia or Genoa.

When we discovered that the stories of the landings were false, we passed through a period of wishful thinking. We took the view that if the Allies had not yet landed in the north, it would not be long before they did so, and it would therefore be a mistake to go south. Gradually the true situation made itself clear. The Allies were not going to make any landings in the north; the only thing to do was either to go south and try to reach our lines, or to go north into Switzerland. Some reacted more quickly than others. I am afraid that Ronald and I were among the last to move, finally starting south on 1 November.

We left the road we had found soon after leaving Lucia's house, and walked for an hour across some very rough country before hitting the road once more. There seemed to be no traffic, so we decided to stick to the highway. We passed through several villages, and in each one we were given a hearty welcome by the inhabitants. Despite the late hour, there were a number of people in each village sitting at tables outside the bars drinking wine. They called to us to stop and insisted that we sit down with them and have a drink. They were all in very good spirits, pro-British to a man and absolutely confident that the British would soon arrive and that everything would be all right. Everyone insisted on standing us drinks, with the result that we consumed a considerable quantity of wine. As it got later, the people disappeared inside their houses, leaving the village streets deserted. The last Italians we spoke to that night were an Italian Air Force officer with his wife and sister-in-law. The officer had deserted in order to avoid capture by the Germans, and was lying low until the British arrived. I fear that he must have had a long wait.

Soon after midnight we reached a point where we had to abandon the road and take to the mule tracks over the mountains. Suddenly a figure stepped out in front of us. It turned out to be Tom Vickers, the other Fontanellato officer from my regiment. He had lost his partner during the mad scramble over the Via Emilia and was continuing his journey alone. He agreed to join up with us. Tom spoke good Italian, which was a great advantage to us as at that time Ronald and I were far from fluent. The three of us walked over the mountains for several hours; it seemed that we were going further and further away from civilization.

By three o'clock in the morning we had climbed to a considerable height, and I must confess that I had no idea of our whereabouts. We were beginning to get rather desperate when we hit the Fidenza–Bardi road and all was well. We decided that we had walked far enough and would stop at the next farmhouse. We walked on down the road and soon saw a farm perched on top of a hill to our right. We climbed the hill, entered the farmyard and looked around for a barn to sleep in. We soon found one, and after drinking some water from a trough we climbed a ladder and settled ourselves down in the straw. We were lulled to sleep by the steady crunch-crunch of the cows as they chewed the cud in the stalls beneath us. We were awakened at dawn by the noise of one of the farmhands milking the cows, and we decided that it was time to make our presence known to the owner of the farm. There was also the important matter of breakfast to be attended to.

As we slid down the ladder we were met by an old woman carrying a pail. We expected her to be surprised and perhaps annoyed at three disreputable-looking men suddenly descending from her loft, but she seemed to regard it as a perfectly normal event and welcomed us in the most friendly manner. We explained to her who we were and asked her if we could wash and shave at the trough. She was perfectly agreeable to this and invited us in for breakfast as soon as we were ready.

The farm, quite a large one, was chiefly devoted to cows. The view from the house was one of the finest I saw during the whole time I was in Italy. The mountains stretched as far as the eye could see, and the colouring on that bright September morning was very beautiful.

We had a refreshing wash and then walked up some steps to the cottage living room. The old lady gave us a delicious meal, and sat and talked to us while we ate. She told us that a priest who lived a few hundred yards away would show us the best way across the hills to Bardi. After breakfast we took leave of our charming old hostess and were conducted to the priest's house by her grandson. The priest took us to a position from where we could see the hills near Bardi. He doubted whether we would be able to reach our destination that night, but assured us that we would have no difficulty in finding lodging for the night *en route.*

We set off across some very rough country, and as the day advanced we stripped to the waist. We passed several farms; at some of them we stopped for a glass of milk or water and everyone was most kind and friendly. By lunchtime we had reached the small town of Varsi, which is about six miles by road from Bardi. We had travelled the whole way across country and were extremely tired and hot. We entered the outskirts of Varsi and got some water to drink. Our appearance caused quite a stir among the inhabitants, who flocked round us asking innumerable questions that only Tom could understand.

A little later, we came across the river which runs up the valley to Bardi. It looked so inviting that we decided to sit down, have our lunch and then a bathe. We chose a shady spot under a tree, ate, and went to sleep. When we awoke, we found ourselves surrounded by a small crowd of *contadini,* who were regarding us as if we were strange creatures.

In nearly every village we visited there were one or two people who spoke English, and whenever we arrived the people insisted that we should wait until the local linguist arrived on the scene. The Italians regarded English and American as two entirely different languages, and we were often asked if we understood American!

On this occasion, the *contadini* informed us that there were two people down the road who spoke English and that they would be coming along in a few minutes. It was very kind of them, but the last thing we wanted to do was to speak to anyone. We wanted to take off our clothes and have a bathe, but with an admiring crowd of Italian girls standing by, this was somewhat difficult. Eventually we took turns to answer the innumerable questions, and the two 'off duty' went further down stream for a swim.

We moved on soon after four o'clock, but were waylaid by the oldest inhabitant of the village. He had worked for twenty years in Hammersmith, London and insisted that we should go to his house. It was impossible to refuse the old man as he was so very kind, and whenever he talked about England his eyes filled with tears. We sat with him and his family for some time and drank wine in a rather dirty and flyridden parlour.

In the meantime, news of our arrival had spread to the other houses and more people came down to have a look at us. Among the newcomers was the local electrician, a young man dressed in a magnificent plum-coloured uniform piped with gold braid. He owned a speedy-looking, plum-coloured bicycle with the tools of his trade strapped on the back. When we told him that it was our intention to go to Giuseppe Dotti at Monastero, he assured us that he knew him well and that he would go off on his bicycle and warn him of our arrival. This seemed an excellent plan, so off he sped in a cloud of dust bearing a note from me to Dotti telling him that we should be arriving some time on the morrow.

We decided to walk on until dark and then find somewhere to sleep, hoping to reach Monastero by lunchtime the next day. We followed the line of the river as far as we could, eventually coming out again on the main Bardi road. Here we stopped until it grew darker, as we feared to walk down the road in daylight. While we were resting, a girl and some children brought us a basket of tomatoes and apples and remained staring at us while we ate them. The girl took a great fancy to Ronald and insisted on walking with him when we started off again. Tom and I followed behind, poking fun at Ronald. A steep hill put an end to this romance, and Ronald's young lady returned to her house.

The night was pleasantly cool and we made excellent progress, but the sight of a comfortable-looking public house proved too much for us. While we were drinking our wine on the porch, an agitated Italian rushed up and informed us that a telephone message had come through telling him that a German patrol had just left Varsi in a truck and was coming our way. We immediately left the road and climbed up the mountainside in search of a farm to spend the night. We soon came to a small house outside which two old women were spinning wool. They agreed to let us sleep in their barn, although it was apparent that they were rather nervous of the Germans. We promised to leave at dawn the next day, and in view of our impending early start, we went straight off to the barn and were soon asleep.

We left the house just after dawn the next morning and struck off across the mountains in the direction of Bardi. We were not very fit, and the last two days of walking had made us very lackadaisical. Instead of reaching Monastero by lunchtime, as we had hoped, we got only as far as the little village of Tosca. Here we met a man who for many years had been a vegetable cook at the Savoy Hotel. For the last ten years he had been in Paris, but he had to leave France at the outbreak of war and bought his small farm at Tosca, where he lived with his wife and daughter.

Our new friend, whose name was Bernardo Gianelli, took us off to his little house and gave us an excellent lunch. Afterwards, he walked with us for some distance until we reached yet another farm with English-speaking people. Here we had to answer another barrage of questions and drink more wine. A young girl gave me a letter to her parents, who lived in Shepherds Bush, and I promised to deliver it when I reached home. How optimistic we were in those days!

The other inmates of the farm gave us several loaves of bread, and eventually we set off once more towards Monastero, which we reached at 5 p.m., after a very tiring walk. Before we reached Dotti's house we stopped at two others on the outskirts of the village. The first was owned by a family of the name of Piggi. All four sons were deserters from the Italian army, and we became great friends with them during our stay in the Monastero district. The second house belonged to Giacomo Restighini, a widower who lived with his daughter Maria and son Lazarino. Giacomo had lived in America for some years and spoke quite good English. It turned out that he was Dotti's uncle, so we asked him to take us to Dotti's house.

Ronald and I had found Lucia so kind and friendly that we imagined her brother would be the same, but in this we were to be disappointed. Immediately we met Dotti and his wife, we got the impression that they were frightened and that we were not exactly *personae gratae.* They received us very politely and provided us with an enjoyable meal, but all the time we had the feeling that they were longing for us to go. We explained to them that we wanted to stay near Monastero in order to listen to the BBC broadcasts until such time as we could join our own troops. Dotti was quite willing to let us listen to the broadcasts on his wireless every night, but he said that it was impossible to put us up. He had only a small house, and as he had three children there was no room available.

We realized that we had drawn a blank as far as the Dottis were concerned. Lucia had courage, but her brother had none. The wireless was the important thing; if only we could find somewhere to stay in the neighbourhood. The Dottis were above the *contadino* class, and it was evident from their house and style of living that they had a certain amount of money. But money in Italy did not spell hope. We were to discover during the next three months that the richer people were, the less they would help us. They had too much to lose. The poorer the people, the greater their help and generosity.

We were wondering what our next move should be when a man named Giacomo came to the rescue. He had a small restaurant attached to his house, but it was closed for the duration of the war. Giacomo said that he had an empty room in which we could sleep. Dotti seemed very relieved, and agreed that we could go to his house any night after dark to listen to the radio.

We returned to Giacomo's house and sat in his parlour while Maria prepared our room. The room was used for storing chestnuts, but there was an old bed in the corner on which one of us could sleep, while the other two used the straw that Maria had put in the other corner of the room. A washbasin and a towel horse completed the furniture.

Having slept in barns and on haystacks for the last three nights, our new apartment seemed positively luxurious. In addition, Giacomo was so genuinely friendly and anxious to please that he made us feel very welcome. We felt lucky to have struck such a good family. Maria was a particularly nice girl and Lazarino the most pleasant boy that we met during our time in Italy.

The fourth member of the household was Angelina, the servant girl. I have always connected the name Angelina with angels, but anyone less like an angel to look at than Angelina would be hard to imagine. Her resemblance to a horse was at times quite startling. Horse or no horse, Angelina had a heart of gold and a lovely mane of shining auburn hair.

After dining with Giacomo we walked over to Dotti's house and listened to the British broadcast. We at last discovered that the landings in the north were fairy tales and that the Germans were still in possession of Naples, though the Allies had made a successful landing at Salerno. As far as we were concerned, the picture had changed completely. Giacomo asked us what we thought was going to happen and we immediately embarked on a voyage of wishful thinking. Naples would soon fall, other landings would take place and the road to Rome would be easy. It would only be a question of a month, or five weeks at the outside. Giacomo shook his head. It would take longer than that. How right he was!

We spent the next three days with Giacomo, walking over each evening to Dotti's house to hear the news. During the day we helped Giacomo and his son to cart wood from the mountain slope.

Monastero was situated on the side of a mountain looking south-west across a valley, with a higher range of mountains on the other side. The road from Bardi came to a dead end below the village – a fortunate thing for us as it meant that there was very little traffic passing anywhere near us. We could see Bardi from the top of the hill. It looked quite an attractive place, with an old, Austrian-built castle rising up in the centre of it. Bardi was the main town in the district, and served as a general meeting place on market day. The mountains above Giacomo's house were covered with oak and chestnut trees; chestnuts played an important part in the national diet during the war.

All the farms around Bardi were smallholdings, each farmer owning a vineyard and strips on the mountainside. There was little grazing land, but the children drove the cattle and sheep up the hill where they picked up what they could from the trees and scrub. All the transport was drawn by oxen, and in the hills a wooden sledge replaced wheels. Very few sheep were reared, but each family kept one, the wool being hand spun by the women of the family.

The pig was an important member of the family. He was kept until January and then, when he was killed, every available piece of him is used – even the ears, to make ersatz soap.

The average *contadino* owned a cow, two oxen and a few chickens. Thus he was practically self-supporting. The pig supplied enough bacon and salami for a year; the cow provided the milk, cheese and butter; the sheep the wool; the vineyards the wine; and any haulage work was done by the two oxen. In addition, the *contadino* usually had a small field of maize and of wheat, from which he obtained flour for the bread which he always baked himself.

The war really affected the *contadini* very little, although they used to pretend that they were undergoing great hardship. They always had plenty to eat and drink, and rationing did not affect them. There was an active black market in meat – calves were usually killed at eight or nine weeks old and the veal sold among friends under cover of darkness.

The *contadini*'s only justifiable complaint was the lack of clothes and footwear. It was practically impossible to procure boots or shoes, and clothes, which cost a ridiculous amount, were of extremely poor quality. As a result, the *contadini* wore rags during the week, keeping their only presentable clothes for Sunday. All their boots had thick wooden soles.

This was the life and these the people among whom we found ourselves in that September of 1943. They were simple folk, and most of them were only too pleased that we should share their life with them.

We decided to stay on another three weeks, hoping that by then something would have happened to clarify the position. After we had been with Giacomo for three days a platoon of Germans arrived at Bardi, and although they only spent the day there they caused much uneasiness among those *contadini* who were sheltering British officers. Signora Dotti was the first to panic, and it was obvious that even Giacomo was uneasy. He wanted to go on helping us, but he was afraid of spies.

Fascism in Italy, like National Socialism in Germany, caused each man to distrust his neighbour. For twenty years the Italians had been forced to swallow Fascism, and although many of them had been anti-Fascist, very few dared to admit it. The situation was aptly described to me by an Italian: 'If you asked a hundred Italians if they were pro-Fascist, they would all say yes. If you asked ten Italians the same question the answer would still be the same. But if you were to take *one* Italian by himself and ask him if he was really a Fascist, he would almost certainly answer in the negative.'

Even in a small village like Monastero, where everyone knew each other, there was the same distrust. Someone might be a spy; he might inform the Fascists in Bardi that the *contadini* were helping British officers, and then they would be shot.

Despite his fear, Giacomo was determined to go on helping us. He was supported in this intention by the one woman in Monastero, and one of the few in Italy, who did not give a damn for spies, Mussolini, Hitler and the whole Fascist régime. This remarkable old lady was Giacomo's aunt, Zia Luiga.

Zia Luiga was a tough old battle-axe of seventy-three, with a heart of gold and a tongue that would silence a Thames bargee. She had often been in trouble with the Fascists because of her outspoken views on Mussolini, whom she always referred to as 'that son-of-a-bitch'. But she had managed to keep out of prison, probably because of her age, and she continued her anti-Fascist campaign. She had lived in America years before, but had forgotten most of her English. 'Son-of-a-bitch' was her favourite expression when she was angry about anyone or anything.

Zia Luiga was very small and frail to look at, but she was as strong as an ox, and inside her wiry old body beat the stoutest heart in Italy. She always wore black and had a dark blue handkerchief fixed like a cape over her head. Her face was a mass of wrinkles, she had not a tooth in her head, and her small dark eyes flashed like shining beads. When she talked – and how she talked! – her voice was a very high-pitched cackle like the witch in *Snow White and the Seven Dwarfs*. Perhaps I have made her sound a rather terrifying person, but this was not the case. Behind all this, one saw immediately the great kindness of her heart. I think she was very fond of me; I certainly was of her. When I met her each day, I used to throw my arms around her and kiss her hand. She used to pretend that she was shy of these affectionate greetings, but she really rather enjoyed them.

'No, no, Filippo, bad Filippo', she used to say, as she pretended to push me away.

When the spy mania started, Giacomo suggested that we should go and live in his *casetta* on the mountainside and come down at night to listen to the radio. A *casetta* was a small hut built of stones, which the *contadini* used for storing leaves and chestnuts.

We readily agreed to this proposal, and the following morning we collected our belongings and set off up the mountain with Dotti and Giacomo. Zia Luiga gave us two pillows and a blanket; Giacomo and Dotti also gave us a blanket, a stew pot and other odds and ends. Maria gave us a basket full of bread, cheese and wine, to which Luiga added eggs and another bottle of wine. Signora Dotti also supplied bread, and an English-speaking woman called Aida gave us wine and salami. We arranged that when we had finished our provisions we would return for more, at the same time listening to the BBC.

We trekked off up the mountain, following a small path that passed through chestnut trees and along the side of a ravine. After walking for forty minutes we came to a small stream, by the side of which stood our *casetta*. The little grey house was well concealed, and it was very unlikely that anyone would find us there.

The *casetta* was about ten feet square, with an arched roof of stone slabs. There were no windows, and no door in the doorway. The floor had a thick covering of leaves. We soon set to work and cleaned these out, replacing them with stone slabs from the stream. Jacko and Dotti left us hard at work, and promised to come and visit us in the morning.

Trees and bracken surrounded the *casetta*, and we cut the bracken to make bedding. We then fixed up a fireplace in the corner of the hut, trusting that the smoke would find a way out through the roof. There was ample wood nearby to keep us supplied with fuel.

There was just enough room on the floor for the three of us to lie abreast with our feet stretched towards the fireplace. The bedding was very hard, but considering everything we managed to sleep fairly well. It was refreshing to be able to get up in the morning and wash in the stream outside. In many ways, it was a relief to get away from the village and not to feel that we were causing anxiety to Giacomo and his friends. The weather was still warm and the scenery round the *casetta* was delightful.

The *casetta* was a good half hour's pull up from Monastero, but there were several small villages on the other side of the mountain within easy walking distance of our new home. We decided to try to find friends in these villages, in order to relieve Monastero of some of the strain of our keep. So the following morning Tom Vickers set off in the direction of Bardi while Ronald and I went to the other side of the mountain.

The first farm we came to was owned by Celeste Pesca, who before the war had worked in the kitchens of the Connaught Rooms. He owned a very pretty farm, where he lived with his wife, mother-in-law, sister-in-law and small daughter. Pesca welcomed us warmly, and we were soon sitting in his parlour drinking wine. He was very pro-British and described Mussolini as a man 'who had tried to be a ———— Napoleon, but had failed'. After that we always referred to Pesca as 'Napoleon'.

I left Ronald with Pesca and walked down the hill to the little village of Noceta. Here I found many friends, who proved so kind and loyal that we eventually shifted our headquarters from Monastero to Noceta. The first man I met was Eugene Gandolfino, who had formerly worked in London, at the Wandsworth Bakery, Vauxhall Bridge Road. 'Wandsworth', as we later named him, proved to be the best of many good friends.

Our first stop was at the house of Giuseppe Negri, a mosaic worker from Paris, which he had left at the outbreak of war. Although Italian, Negri was much more like a Frenchman in his mannerisms, clothes and habits. A widower aged about fifty-five, he lived in his little house with two grown-up sons and his house-keeper, the prettiest girl in the village. Negri loved good food and wine and he provided us with a better meal than anyone else in the district. He was also the proud possessor of a small wireless on which we could listen to the BBC. In addition he owned a loft full of fresh dry straw, and said we could sleep there whenever we wished. Negri and I became great friends and I spent many enjoyable evenings at his house.

In the next house to Negri lived Aldo Barbuti with his wife, three children, his mother and his sister Mariella. They spoke no English, but invited us to their house whenever we wished to go there.

Noceta was a very small village and these three families were the chief personalities of the place, though there were several others who were also extremely good to us.

In the evening, I returned to the *casetta* to report to Ronald and Tom on the success of my mission. Tom had also made good progress, while Ronald had already become a great favourite with Napoleon. We decided to get food from the three districts in turn, one week going to Monastero, another to Noceta, and another to Tom's friends. In this way, we felt we were not being a burden to anyone. We used to go twice a week to listen to the radio at Dotti's, spending the night with either Luiga or Giacomo, and twice a week to Negri's, sleeping at night in his barn. They all gave us ample supplies, and on Sundays we were always asked to lunch at one house or another.

The warm weather continued until the end of September and life in our *casetta* was quite pleasant. We used to wander over the mountains during the day and do odd jobs, such as chopping wood for our fire. We found a lot of mushrooms on the hillside, and these supplied us with a fine delicacy for supper in the shape of mushroom soup – until one day we ate some bad ones; after that we gave the mushrooms a miss.

The beginning of October brought an unwelcome change in the weather. It became very cold at night and rained during the day. Life in the *casetta* became most unpleasant, as the roof leaked, and in order to keep warm at night, we had to keep the fire going the whole time. We realized that there was now very little hope of an Allied landing and that sooner or later we would have to move south or go to Switzerland.

We visited the priest in Monastero and he lent us a map from which to copy the route south. There was just a chance that we might get a boat to take us over to Corsica, and we decided to try this before moving. Tom Vickers had an aunt who owned a villa near Rapallo. The gardener and his wife still occupied the villa, and Tom suggested that he should try to get in touch with them and ask them to make enquiries about a boat, and also to get us more clothes and money.

On 15 October, Tom set off on his journey, stating that if he was not back by 1 November we must not wait for him.

While Tom was away the situation in the Monastero district became increasingly difficult. A constant stream of escaped prisoners of every nationality, including Yugoslavs, Greeks and Russians, were passing through the district. The Fascist régime was reorganizing itself, and the *contadini* were becoming increasingly nervous of spies and Germans. Dotti and his wife were the first to show signs of uneasiness, which gradually had an effect on Giacomo. He wanted to help but was worried about his family. Old Luiga kept calm and said that we could sleep in her house whenever we wanted. Napoleon was anxious but continued to ask us to meals. Negri and Wandsworth remained completely calm and said that the spy menace was a lot of rubbish and that as far as they were concerned, we could spend the winter with them. Evenings in the village became impossible, as in the middle of supper someone would inevitably rush in to say that the Fascists were coming, whereupon we would be hustled out into the night to find our way back to the *casetta* – a dangerous and difficult undertaking in the dark.

Tom arrived back on 29 October. He had been unsuccessful in his search for a boat and had been unable to reach his aunt's house because of the number of Germans in the district. He had managed to get two women to go to the house for him, armed with a letter to the gardener. They had returned with clothing and four thousand lire. Tom very kindly gave Ronald and me a civilian shirt and vest and a thousand lire each.

I shall never forget the night that Tom arrived back. I met him at Giacomo's for supper, and Ronald went to dine and sleep at Napoleon's. Tom and I were going to sleep at Luiga's. We were having a pleasant supper with Giacomo when suddenly we were warned that the Bardi Fascists were on their way to the village. Giacomo went very white, and even the placid Maria looked worried. We took a lantern from Giacomo and set off to walk back to the *casetta*. In the meantime, Ronald had been pushed out of Napoleon's house. Marietta and the girls had rushed up from Noceta to warn him of the danger.

We all arrived back at the *casetta* in a very bad temper, determined to leave the district as soon as possible. The evening had started badly, but worse was to follow. The night was cold, so we kept a good fire going. It was my turn to act as stoker for the night. I looked at the fire at three in the morning and decided that I could pile on enough fuel to last until dawn. I then went off to sleep with the satisfactory feeling that I would not have to get up again to attend to the fire. But within an hour I awoke to find the *casetta* full of smoke and the roof on fire. I had piled the logs too high and the flames had set light to the wooden beam in the roof. I woke up Ronald and Tom and we stumbled out into the night with our bucket to get water from the stream. We soon had the fire under control, and after pulling half the roof off we managed to extinguish the burning beam.

Any further sleep was impossible, and we waited miserably for dawn to break. Breakfast then had to be cooked, and while the other two were washing I went off to get some wood. Before going, I hung my woollen vest – my most treasured possession – on the roof to air. When I arrived back I found a cow standing outside the *casetta* munching my vest with a look of intense pleasure on its ridiculous face. The arm of my vest was hanging from the animal's mouth, and the rest of the garment had been chewed to a pulpy mess. With a shout of anguish I seized my ruined vest and hit the astonished animal as hard as I could across its backside with a spade. At this juncture a small boy who was supposed to be looking after the cow appeared on the scene. I shouted every obscene Italian word I could think of, and threw in a few good English oaths to indicate to the frightened little boy what I thought of him and his cow. He was most upset and when tears appeared in his eyes I almost forgave him. We then spent the next few minutes chasing the cow and hurling every available missile at the terrified animal. Thanks to the change of underclothes which Tom had brought me from Rapallo, the situation was not as serious as it might have been.

We spent the last two days of October making preparations for our departure. Tom had decided to make for Switzerland, and Ronald and I were going south to try to reach the Allied lines. Ronald had completed his maps, and we had also managed to get some motoring maps from Dotti. We found a guide to take us over the river Taro, the first major obstacle; he had already successfully taken several other parties over this route.

At the last moment, an ex-Italian soldier from Noceta, Giovanni Ferrabosci, announced his intention of coming with us. He had fought in the Abyssinian war and had been wounded in the leg. He now decided that he would join Badoglio's troops in the south. Giovanni was much tougher than the average Italian, and we thought he might be a useful companion. He was rather a strange man and gave us the impression that his words were greater than his deeds. Wandsworth told us that he was perfectly honest but that it was unlikely he would stay with us for more than four or five days. We did not mind that, as all we wanted was to have someone with us at the start of our journey.

We arranged to spend the last night in Negri's barn so that we could be near our guide for an early start in the morning. Our last lunch at the *casetta* was a wonderful affair. Dear old Zia Luiga walked up the long slope from Monastero carrying on her head a basket full of roast chicken, bread and wine. Her lunatic brother accompanied her, carrying a second bottle of wine. The walk from Monastero used to make us feel tired, but old Luiga arrived as fresh as paint, despite the heavy basket. It was the last of her many kind deeds and one I shall never forget.

There were many goodbyes to be said before we left Noceta, and we spent the last afternoon visiting all our friends in the district. When we said goodbye to Napoleon, his wife and mother burst into floods of tears, and I felt like having a good cry myself. One could not help being moved by the loyalty and affection which these big-hearted people had shown us. From Napoleon we went on to Giacomo's and here again we had a tender if rather embarrassing farewell. Giacomo and Maria were on the verge of tears, and even old Luiga showed signs of emotion. I thought we were going to get away without any actual weeping, when suddenly the mad brother started to howl and implored us not to go. I put my arm round him, as one would with a child, and promised that we could come back soon. Luiga then announced that he was not crying because I was leaving but simply because I was wearing his hat!

We then went on to see the Dottis, Aida, the priest, and finally to Noceta, where we were to spend the night. By this time, we were loaded with provisions that our friends had given us at parting. If we had accepted all the gifts they had offered us, we would have needed a horse and cart to carry them.

When we got to Noceta, Tom Vickers left us, as he was going to walk over to Tosca where he was to spend the night with our friend from the Savoy. I was very sorry to see him go, as we had had great fun together. We arranged that whoever reached their goal first should get in touch with our families in England. Tom reached

Switzerland safely and arrived back to England in October 1944.

We had a farewell party with Wandsworth, Negri and the Barbuttis. After an excellent dinner, we retired to the loft earlier than usual as we had arranged to meet our guide at eight the following morning at his house in the next village.

October had been a very wet month, and when I settled down in the straw that night I prayed for good weather. My prayers were answered, as when we climbed down from the loft the next morning the sky was bright blue and a brilliant sun was appearing over the mountain.

Giovanni Ferrabosci met us at the Barbuttis' house wearing a thick grey overcoat and carrying a suitcase, a stick, and his few belongings wrapped in a towel. We stuffed the suitcase with the bread and other food we had been given. Giacomo had presented me with a blanket, in which I rolled up my washing things and a spare shirt. I then tied the bundle with a pink dressing-gown cord which Mariella had given me and slung it over my shoulder like a pack. I also carried an Italian haversack, which contained the notebooks of my second attempt at this story and a few loaves of bread.

Three days later I found a note in my pocket from Mariella, our Italian teacher. I have it before me now:

Dear Filippo and Ronaldo,

I promise to pray always for both of you. I am so very sad. Every day at two o'clock your teacher will still wait for you. Really I will. I send you every good wish and hope to see you after the war, if you have not forgotten me. I will never forget.

Your Italian Teacher

And so I end this chapter. Though I have called it 'Seven wasted weeks', when I look back on the many friends we made during that period and all the kindness we enjoyed, I begin to wonder if they were wasted after all.

6

The road south

The sun was shining from a bright blue sky when we left our guide's house and began our ascent of the mountain. On the other side lay the little town of Ostia, where we had decided to cross the river Taro. It was a saint's day, dedicated to the beautification of all the graveyards in Italy. As we passed, the peasants paused awhile from their back-breaking job to stare at us.

The ascent was extremely steep and the going very rough. Our guide went along at a good pace, occasionally looking back over his shoulder to see if we were keeping up. I, too, kept looking back, back towards the little villages in the valley and on the side of the hill towards Bardi. Everything seemed so very peaceful, and the silence of the mountainside was broken only by the tinkle of cowbells or the shrill cry of a girl calling to the oxen. The ascent seemed endless, but after climbing for two hours we reached the summit, and much to my relief our guide suggested a rest.

After sending final messages of farewell to Negri and our other friends, we took our last look at Monastero and Noceta and then continued our way across the plateau before making the descent to Ostia. We soon saw the river Taro, cutting its way through the valley below, accompanied on one side by a railway and on the other by the main road to Borgo Taro. The river seemed to be in fair flood, and hopes of crossing it other than by bridge soon vanished from our minds. The problem of the railway was easily solved, as just above Ostia the line ran through a tunnel. There seemed to be very little traffic on the main road, so we felt that once over the river bridge our main difficulty would be solved.

We reached a village about a quarter of a mile above Ostia, and here we stopped at a public house to quench our thirst and to find out all we could regarding the situation at Ostia. While we were in the village, a large force of Allied planes flew over on their way to bomb Spezia. We could hear the bombs dropping in the distance and later saw the planes returning.

We were told that there were a few Germans at Ostia, but that most of them spent their time guarding the station. It was unfortunate for us that we had struck a saint's day, as it meant that more people than usual would be walking about doing nothing. Our plan was to walk within two hundred yards of the bridge and then sit down on the side of the hill and observe. When a suitable moment arrived, Giovanni and I were to walk ahead and cross the bridge. When Ronald saw us safely across the bridge and the main road he was to follow, and meet us in the woods the other side. The guide was to see us all across and then return home. Although he would not get back until nightfall, he absolutely refused to take any payment, insisting that it was a pleasure and an honour to be of help.

Immediately Giovanni and I saw the bridge and its surroundings clear of people, we bid goodbye to our guide and set off. We must have looked rather peculiar. Giovanni was dressed in his immense overcoat and was carrying the suitcase and his towelful of odds and ends. I had my haversack and blanket-roll on my back. We were bound to attract attention on a saint's day, when everyone was dressed in his best clothes and sitting back doing nothing.

Just as we arrived at the bridge, three men appeared at the other end. They were not of the *contadino* type, and when I saw them my heart dropped to my boots. Giovanni walked ahead. The three men seemed very interested in us and asked what we were doing and where we were going. Giovanni kept on walking and shouted that he was a Roman and that he was going to Rome – a particularly stupid statement. As I passed, the men peered into my face and I expected them at any moment to call for the Germans at the station. Once we were over the bridge, we darted across the main road, into the wood on the other side, and on up the hill. Giovanni went faster and faster and I felt hotter and hotter. Finally, I shouted to him that we must sit down and wait for Ronald, who soon appeared, having made the crossing without interruption.

Giovanni said that we should push on as far as we could that night as it was *molto pericoloso* to stay anywhere near Ostia. We soon learned that Giovanni thought everything was *molto pericoloso* unless he was perched on top of a mountain miles from anyone. However, we thought he would be useful until we had found our feet and discovered the best methods to adopt on our journey. In addition, he was carrying the suitcase full of food, and we wished to retain him until that was empty!

We walked on until five o'clock that evening and reached an isolated farmhouse. We were given a frigid reception by the mistress of the house – the only occasion during our trip through Italy that we were badly received by *contadini*. Perhaps it was the sight of Giovanni. He certainly was a villainous-looking creature.

It was getting dark, and the thought of any more walking depressed me more than words could describe. At that moment, an old man appeared with three mules. He owned a barn on the farm and he said he would be delighted if we would sleep there. We gratefully accepted his invitation, and sat down on the steps to eat our supper.

We passed an excellent night and set off soon after dawn the following morning. It was raining slightly, and there was a thick mist which made walking very unpleasant. The higher we climbed, the worse the mist became. Giovanni assured us that he knew exactly where he was and that we should soon cross the main La Spezia road below the Chisa Pass. We discovered that the maps Ronald had made with such care were now useless, as our guide had started off miles to the west of our intended route. Giovanni was so confident that we decided to follow him blindly.

We were following a narrow mountain path when suddenly a church tower loomed out of the mist. This seemed to give Giovanni rather a shock and he immediately announced that the situation was *molto pericoloso*. Then we heard the noise of motor transport going down a road ahead of us. Giovanni bore left and led us through some bushes. The next thing we knew we were standing within ten yards of a German anti-aircraft listening post!

The situation was definitely *molto pericoloso*, and we retreated in the opposite direction. It turned out that Giovanni had lost his bearings and had led us straight into the Chisa Pass. We went left with the intention of crossing the road lower down. Just as we were approaching the road, two German trucks came swinging down from La Chisa. We threw ourselves on the grass and prayed to God that we would not be seen. All went well – the trucks drove on and we nipped across the road.

As we walked along the mountainside by La Chisa, we saw holes in the ground where the German soldiers had been practising mortar fire. We had certainly been much too close to danger on this second day, and we decided to try to keep Giovanni more under control. Soon after we had crossed the pass, the sun broke through the mist and we found ourselves amid glorious mountain scenery with the La Spezia road twisting its way through the mountains in the distance.

The third day of our journey was the most tiring and exasperating day that I have ever spent. Giovanni assured us that he knew the way and proceeded to lead us up the side of a particularly steep mountain. Owing to a very early start, we had had no breakfast and soon discovered that mountain climbing on an empty stomach was no fun. It was a glorious day, and by nine o'clock the sun was very hot. We reached the top of the first hill in an exhausted condition and decided to rest for half an hour and eat some breakfast from Giovanni's now half-empty suitcase.

We continued our journey up and down, up and down, with the paths getting rougher by the hour. Eventually we reached a point overlooking Pontremoli. There were two alternatives open to us: to go down to the plain leaving Pontremoli on our right, or to go straight ahead which meant climbing another fifteen hundred feet. I was in favour of going by the plain, which seemed by far the shortest and easiest route. Giovanni immediately said it would be *molto pericoloso* to do so, and much to my annoyance Ronald backed him up. I was in a very bad temper and nearly went off on my own. Eventually I agreed to their plan and we started another dreary climb. Just as we approached the summit, Giovanni announced that he could see an anti-aircraft gun on the top and that we would have to go round. We looked to where he pointed and saw an object that remotely resembled an old cannon. By this time, my temper was nearly out of control and I told Giovanni not to be a fool. How could anyone put a gun on top of a mountain? Giovanni replied that the Germans did this to get nearer the aeroplanes! We both started to laugh at him, when suddenly he became even more excited. He could see soldiers moving by the gun. There certainly were some moving figures, but they proved on closer inspection to be sheep, and the anti-aircraft gun a fallen tree!

We continued along the top of the ridge. The going got worse and the only good part of the walk was the view. As the afternoon advanced the wind became very cold, and it was obvious that we were completely lost. The situation was looking very black when suddenly we saw two men walking towards us. Giovanni hailed them and they turned out to be two Italian deserters who lived in the district. They had come up the mountain in search of something to shoot and asked us what we were doing on such a deserted peak. It turned out that we had come completely out of our way and that we should have gone by the plain. There was nothing for it but to walk down the side of the mountain again, which our friends said would take at least three hours. They pointed out the best way to the nearest village and we began the steep descent.

After three hours of walking, we found signs of civilization in the shape of a man and two boys counting sheep in a pen. They agreed to guide us to the village, where we found an excellent public house and sat down to eat and drink. We finished five litres of wine in the public house and then moved on to another house in the village where we were to spend the night. The villagers were most friendly, and before the night was out we had finished eight litres of wine between us. It was a great party and by the time I went to sleep in the hay I had forgotten all the misfortunes of the day.

We had arranged to start off at four in the morning because Giovanni was nervous about the village people, and we all awoke with terrific hangovers. Giovanni was in a very bad way. We walked until midday, when we reached the little village of Tavarnelle. Giovanni was showing signs of distress and announced that his leg was hurting him. Ronald and I were feeling the effects of the night before, so we decided to stop in Tavarnelle until the next day. Giovanni announced that he could go no further because of his leg.

Before we left Tavarnelle, Ronald and I managed to get fairly accurate directions about the best way through the mountains to Florence. Our intention was to travel the whole way using the mule track through the mountains, only touching the roads when it was absolutely necessary. Thanks to the topography of Italy, with the Apennines running from north to south, this was not difficult. The mountains were dotted with small villages connected by mule tracks, most of which were many miles from a main road. Our plan was to walk each day from eight in the morning until three-thirty in the afternoon, and then to start looking for somewhere to stay the night.

We said goodbye to Giovanni and gave him many messages for our friends in Noceta. I do not expect that any of them were surprised at his return. It was a great relief to get rid of him and we continued our journey in high spirits. The date was 5 November.

The first stage of our journey was to reach Florence, and the second to reach the British lines in the neighbourhood of Pescara. Our food had run out and we relied entirely on the Italian *contadini* for food and shelter. The route lay through mountains and valleys; thus, to go fifteen miles as the crow flies usually meant walking twenty to twenty-five miles by the mule tracks. During the journey I kept a diary, from which these extracts have been taken.

5 November We made good progress and reached the little village of Po, where we stopped for the night. Ronald was ill but we put it down to something he had eaten.

6 November A glorious day of blue skies and bright sunshine. We lunched at a public house, and during the meal I noticed that Ronald's eyes were very yellow. In the evening we reached the little village of Dali Sopra and we discovered that Ronald had jaundice. We managed to get a double bed in a small annexe of the local public house. The owner said that we must move on in the morning. We slept in the double bed and passed a most uncomfortable night as Ronald was ill at regular intervals.

7 November Ronald was feeling very ill and had turned bright yellow. I managed to persuade the hotelkeeper to let us stay another night. The village was full of evacuees from Livorno.

8 November Ronald was still too ill to move. The weather got colder and colder and the snow became quite deep. How I dislike sleeping in a double bed with a man who has jaundice!

9 November Ronald felt much better so we decided to leave. The hotelkeeper refused to accept any money. We walked on slowly and reached Corfino at teatime. Corfino was a larger place than we had expected, and the Germans were quite near at Castelnuovo. Our host and hostess were very poor but gave us a wonderful supper of minestrone. After supper we went to another house and listened to the BBC news, which relayed a speech by Winston Churchill. I drank plenty of wine and slept well in the old lady's hay loft.

10 November Ronald was much improved, and we walked about twenty miles to Copraia, where we spent the night in another barn.

11 November We reached Fuchandra at midday. Ronald was better, but still very yellow. We were directed to the house of a rich woman who had helped some other officers a week before. She had a friend who was a doctor, and he arrived after lunch to see Ronald. The doctor said that Ronald needed a few days rest. It was impossible to stay in Fuchandra as the Germans were close by, so it was arranged that we would go up the mountain to a lonely farm belonging to a *contadino* family whom our hostess knew.

The walk to the farm was very tiring; it took us over two hours to reach the top of the mountain. We were greeted by Signora Giovanni Bertoncini and her six children. Also at the house was a young Italian officer who was hiding from the Fascists. The farmhouse was somewhat ramshackle but had the most magnificent view across the mountain tops. The family consisted of four girls and two boys, and it was obvious that they resented our presence. Despite the kindness of our host and hostess, I realized at once that our stay was not going to be much fun.

Ronald and I slept in a double bed in a room with the two boys. Most uncomfortable and rather cold.

12 November I spent the morning writing the second version of my story. The family, who were quite uneducated, were amazed at the speed with which I write. In the evening, there was a scare that the Germans were coming up the mountain to examine a plane which had crashed the day before. We were hustled out of the house to a farm lower down, where we slept the night in a hay loft.

13 November Rita (one of the daughters) arrived down before breakfast and announced that the scare was over. The Germans had turned out to be *carabinieri*. We returned to Bertoncini's house.

14 November It poured with rain the entire day. The children nearly drove us mad and we decided to leave the next day. It was Sunday, and in the evening the family had prayers. Ronald and I stood up while the mother recited the Rosary. The rest of the family joined in with *Ave Maria* and *Pater Noster*, but they seemed to pay no attention to the prayers and continued playing draughts.

15 November We left the house at midday and walked to Bachionero, where we slept in a barn. It was a great relief to be out of a double bed!

16 November When we came out of the barn we found there was thick snow on the ground. We relied entirely on the mule tracks to find our way through the mountains, and as these were now covered in snow the question of our route posed rather a problem. We decided to push on, and found that the paths were not as difficult to find as we had expected, so although the going was very hard, we managed to cover a good distance. We spent the night near Montefigatessi, another village perched right on top of a rocky peak.

17 November After breakfast we started up the hill to Montefigatessi. We found two or three people who spoke English, and were directed to a shop where we were told we could get directions for the day's walk. We bought some food and gathered that several other officers had passed through the village a fortnight earlier. Most of the people seemed rather nervous as there were German troops carrying out manoeuvres in the district. We could hear explosions in the distance but it was difficult to locate the exact position of the enemy. The weather had improved considerably but we seemed to make rather slow progress and spent the night in Casoli.

18 November An extremely cold day with more snow on the ground. We were lucky to find a guide to take us over the mountain path. The snow was very thick and it was impossible to make out the tracks.

By the evening, we were in sight of the town of Pistoia. The town was full of Germans so we had to be careful. We had one very narrow escape when looking for a suitable place to cross the road. We came round a corner in the track and practically bumped into a German working party. Luckily, they were just stopping work for the day and we lay low until they moved off in a truck. We spent an uncomfortable night sleeping on a farmhouse floor.

19 November Our host said that he would show us the best way to skirt Pistoia as he was going that way himself. We set off after breakfast and seemed to be walking straight to the town. We had not been so close to a built-up area since we had started, but the only thing was to trust our guide. He took us practically to the outskirts of the town and showed us where to cross the main road. He then left us. There was a lot of traffic and we saw several German staff cars go by. We walked parallel to the road for a while, keeping under the cover of the olive groves.

A farmer told us to follow a boy who was driving some sheep towards the town and to cross the road just short of the aerodrome. We walked along with the boy, helping him with his sheep and trying to look as unconcerned as possible. When we got to the main road, there was a high wall the other side and it was impossible to cross. The boy and the sheep had disappeared and we were left standing in the road. We doubled back and hid ourselves down a side turning. A very frightened girl tried to help us, but she completely lost her head when she heard a car approaching. It was a difficult situation, as people were beginning to collect around us. We went back to the bridge and walked down the river bed, which luckily was practically bereft of water. We were still in full view of the road and it was essential that we acted quickly. An old woman standing in a side turning off the main road had been watching us, and guessing that we were English she signalled to us to come up to where she was standing. She then walked out into the road and, when it was all clear, gave us the signal to cross over. Once we were safely across, she told us to follow her up a narrow path leading to a small wood. The hillside offered little cover, and there were many large houses overlooking the road. The old woman pointed out a large hotel on our left which the German commander of the district was using as his headquarters. Our farmer friend could not have led us to a more dangerous spot. When we got to the wood the old lady told us to keep walking up the hill. We crept along to the edge of the wood and, after two German trucks had passed by, slipped over the road and through a tunnel under the railway embankment. The countryside was more thickly populated and the houses were mostly small villas, painted in bright shades of pink and blue. We kept going up the mountainside as fast as we could, and when we considered ourselves clear of danger we sat down in a thicket and had some food. It had been a very difficult morning.

In the evening, we reached a rich-looking villa. We were given brandy by our nervous host, and also some clothing. We spent the night in a hay loft.

20 November We left the barn shortly before dawn. It was pouring with rain and low clouds were sweeping up the plain on our right towards Pistoia. The mackintosh and overcoat we had been given the night before proved a blessing. We climbed up the mountain, but the rain was so heavy that we decided to stop at the first farm we came to. We soon reached a small farm, where we were welcomed by the *contadini*, who gave us breakfast.

The rain cleared, and we continued on our way in bright sunshine. The scenery was particularly beautiful, but the going hard. We walked over twenty miles and in the evening reached a hill overlooking Prato. The country before us looked dangerous. We were faced with having to cross another main road, a river and a railway. We went down the hill as far as we dared and obtained shelter at a small house some four hundred yards above the main road.

21 November We decided to cross the road and river while it was still dark. We got up well before dawn and started off down the hill, but found we had misjudged the distance. By the time we got to the road it was daylight, and the district showed signs of life. We followed a wood down to the road and climbed over the wall at the bottom. There were several people on the road, and the river in front of us was too deep to wade through. A factory and railway station were just to our left, and a village to our right. We did not know which way to turn. A passing Italian saw that we were in trouble and advised us to give the station a wide berth. He said that we could cross the river further to the right. We walked up the road, trying to look at our ease but failing dismally. We soon found a spot where the river was not too deep and started to wade across. In the last few strides, Ronald fell flat on his face and was soaked through. We went on over the railway and climbed the hill opposite as fast as we could. We were both feeling very tired, so we decided to try and find somewhere to rest until the following morning. We stopped at a very pretty little village called La Briglia.

22 November We were favoured with splendid weather. At lunch time, we stopped at a house for a drink and met a charming old lady whose house in one of the large towns had been bombed. She gave us a salad, and also a mixture of brandy and eggs to drink. She was most dignified and old-fashioned and looked very like Queen Mary. In the evening we reached Bivigliano and spent the night with a *contadini* family of eighteen. The rats in the barn were rather troublesome, but we slept quite well.

24 November We had to get out early as there were Fascists in the village. It was pouring with rain, and as we made our way up into the hills a thick mist descended. I was completely lost and trusted entirely to Ronald's sense of direction. We were making for the old monastery of Montesenario. I was beginning to get worried when the outline of the monastery loomed out of the mist, a tribute to Ronald's good judgement.

The monks did not seem to like the look of us, but we went into the chapel to shelter from the rain. A workman doing repairs gave us directions, and we walked off down the avenue of cypress trees leading from the monastery to the road. Suddenly, the mist cleared, and we could see Florence in the distance. The rain had stopped and the early morning sun emerging through the clouds gave the old city a bright and shining appearance. We stayed in the hills to the north of Florence, reaching the village of Santa Brigida by lunch time. On the way we met four British soldiers who had been in the district for some time. They told us that we could get a useful map from the local priest and that there was a good cobbler in the village who would mend our boots. The priest was quite helpful, though a trifle nervous. We then went to a shop and bought some wine and onions, and a young man gave us some grease for our boots. The news spread that we were in the shop, and a small crowd collected outside. We were just leaving when in walked an English woman, who was married to an Italian. As we were wet through, she suggested we rest in the house of a friend of hers. The rain had started again, so we willingly agreed to the plan, spending the night in a hay loft.

24 November We set off after breakfast on a path that led through olive groves and vineyards. The river Sieve presented a formidable obstacle, but we found a miller who took us over in a boat. We then crossed a main road and railway just to the right of the town of Ruffina. On the way up the mountain, we met a man with an ox cart who gave us a lift up the hill. Our new friend took us to his house for lunch. We then climbed all afternoon and arrived dead beat at a house near Torsino. After supper, we slept in a large cow house. The night was very cold and the heat from the cows and oxen was very welcome, though rather smelly.

25 November I had caught a chill on the previous day and woke up with a streaming cold. We left in pouring rain, but the weather cleared during the morning. I felt very ill, and unfortunately we had difficulty finding anyone to put us up as there were Fascists in the nearby town of Stia. Eventually a very poor *contadino* let us sleep in his barn. Our supper consisted of roast chestnuts and wine.

26 November A lovely frosty morning with bright sunshine. I felt much better. We gave Stia a wide berth, keeping well up the mountain. We saw the village of Poppi in the distance, where there had been a senior officers' camp before the Armistice. We bought cigarettes and wine at shop near a secondary road, but soon after had to dash for shelter when a suspicious-looking car came round the corner. After walking for ten hours, we found it difficult to get lodging for the night, eventually being taken in just before dark. An excellent supper and a comfortable night in the straw.

27 November Very hard going across the mountains to Laverna monastery, where we were given lunch by the Franciscan friars. The old friar who worked in the kitchen told us that they had already given meals to four hundred British officers and men since the Armistice. The village was full of rich evacuees from Rome, who were sympathetic but not helpful. A formation of seventy-five Flying Fortresses passed over just before we left. We reached the village of Capressi that night and slept in the usual barn.

28 November The weather was more like May than November, and the country we passed through delightful. At midday we descended into a valley and crossed the river Tiber. The main road to Rome ran through the valley, so we crossed over as soon as possible. Quite a good by-road wound its way up the hill opposite, and as it appeared to carry no traffic we decided to leave the mule tracks and use this road. Our objective was the small village of Castel Nuovo, perched on a hill in the distance.

When we reached the village we found that it consisted of half a dozen houses, a church and one shop. Just below the village, we passed a large château surrounded by paddocks in which several good-looking horses were grazing. We found a shop, where we bought a bottle of wine, some onions and gherkins, which we ate sitting on the steps of the church. The view was magnificent, as we could follow the Tiber valley for miles.

We were uncertain whether to visit the château until we met the head gamekeeper, dressed in a green uniform and wearing a family crest in his hat. He told us that the château belonged to a Count Galatza and that we were certain of a warm welcome. We both felt much embarrassed as we entered the front door and found ourselves in beautifully furnished apartments. We felt more than ever like tramps, and apologized for our filthy appearance. The countess soon appeared and did everything to make us feel at home. I was still suffering from a cold, so Countess Galatza insisted on giving me a box of aspirin and a small flask of brandy to take with me. She also offered us money, clothes and anything else we required, but we rather stupidly declined her kind offer, regretting our refusal as soon as we had left the house. Before we left we wrote our names in the visitors' book, which contained the names of several officers from Fontanellato including 'Millie', my running trainer. Our host and hostess much regretted that they could not offer to put us up; as they were known anti-Fascists it would obviously have been dangerous. They suggested that we follow the mule track over the hills and spend the night with one of their tenants.

We reached a farm just before dusk and were given a hearty welcome by the *contadini*. After supper, followed by family prayers, we spent a comfortable night with the cattle.

29 November The weather had broken and we set off in a thick mountain mist. The *contadini* gave us instructions regarding the route, but we were soon in difficulties and completely lost. We were soaked through, and as we struggled through brambles and bushes our tempers became progressively worse. After hours of toil, we saw a farmhouse looming out of the mist, and we decided that we had had enough. The owners of the house were a very old man, who was a complete cripple, and an obviously overworked wife. Two sons, both deserters from the Army, were now living with their parents. We explained our situation, and it was agreed that we could spend the rest of the day there and dry our clothes, leaving early the next morning. These people were poor and the food was well below standard, but they were very kind. One of the other sons was in Germany and the mother burst into floods of tears whenever anyone mentioned him. It was a very depressing end to a bad day.

30 November The mist had cleared. The going was steep and very muddy, but we were determined to make up for the time we had wasted yesterday. In the afternoon we stopped at a school in the mountains and were given some wine by the local schoolmistress. Fortified, we finished a ten-hour walk at a little farm above Antirata, where we spent the night.

It was now exactly a month since we had left Noceta. We had walked twenty-three days out of the thirty, and had covered about three hundred and forty miles. Not bad going, but if Ronald had not had jaundice we would have done better. The kindness of the *contadini* had far exceeded our expectations. With very few exceptions, we had been given food and shelter whenever we asked for it. Our method of asking was always the same. I would knock at the door and explain at once to the houseowner that we were two British officers making our way south to join our own troops. We were very tired and could they put us up for the night in their barn? This little speech, delivered in rather bad Italian, nearly always met with a generous response. Most of the *contadini* seemed to regard it as a perfectly natural state of affairs, and told us to come inside. As the evening advanced and the rest of the family (which usually consisted of a dozen or more) came in from the fields, they showed no surprise at seeing us, and by the way they received us we might have been staying in the house for the last month.

Most of the houses were similar. The living room would be a parlour-cum-kitchen with a large open fireplace and an old-fashioned cooking pot hanging from a hook in the chimney. Any frying was done by pulling out red-hot embers from the fire and putting them under a triangular iron stand. The *contadini* were all splendid cooks, and took great pride in the preparation and cooking of their food.

They are most inquisitive people, and we found that we had to answer the same questions night after night. We used to refer to it as 'paying for our supper'. Are you married? How many children do you have? Are your parents living? Where do you live? Are you a regular soldier? How many years' service? What do you do in civilian life? The Germans are bad men, are they not? What about the Russians? When will the war end?

They were very sympathetic about one's wife, and when we mentioned the children, they always exclaimed, '*Ah! poverino!*' (Ah! poor man!). I always caused a stir when I announced that I had five children, one of whom I had never seen.

Like most Italians, the *contadini* make much use of their hands when talking. In fact, if you tied their hands behind their backs I don't think they would be able to talk at all. We got to know all their little mannerisms, some of which were very amusing.

If we were passing a house and one of them asked if we wanted something to eat, he would repeatedly strike the pit of his stomach with the edge of his hand, the palm facing upwards and say '*Avete fame?*' If there were Fascists or Germans in the district, the *contadino* would strike the inside of his right elbow with the open palm of his left hand, at the same time working the right forearm up and down. When referring to Germans, Fascists, Mussolini and Hitler, they would go through the motions of slitting their throats. But if a Fascist or German came within a mile of them, they would run off and hide in the woods. Another method of showing disapproval of someone was to scratch the end of their chins.

The women dressed very much alike; the older ones wore black scarves round their heads, while the younger ones went in for coloured bandannas. Stockings did not exist, and because of the shortage of leather nearly all their boots and shoes were soled with wood. Their working clothes were usually black or grey, but on Sundays they produced quite a splash of colour.

Their life was a hard one, but in comparison to the town worker, a happy one. They worked their own land and lived on the produce, selling the little that was left over to buy clothes and other necessities. One of them summed up his life when he said to me, 'We work to live and we are happy'.

I had been to Italy once or twice before the war, but had never realized the enormous difference between the Italians of the plains and the Italians of the hills. Most of the villages we passed through were only accessible by rough mule track, and were far from roads and railways. I am confident that many English officers and soldiers after the war knew the hills of Italy and its inhabitants a great deal better than do many Italians in the plains. No one can claim really to know Italy until he has walked some hundred miles through the Apennines and experienced the hospitality of the *contadini*.

We must now go on with our journey, which, alas, was soon to come to an abrupt conclusion.

November became December. The weather was cold but fine as we continued our journey. On 2 December the ground was frozen hard and the going slippery, but the sun shone all day. We were somewhat delayed by a difficult river crossing. We stopped the night at a farmhouse near Semonte. The *contadino* and his wife were the most charming we had met on our journey south. Our hosts were a devoted couple and had raised twelve children. The wife was very good looking and appeared remarkably young for her age. The whole family was very cheerful and they all gave us the impression that they were accustomed to living well. One of the married daughters had a small baby who was the pet of the household, the unfortunate little creature being passed from one member of the family to another and smothered with their caresses. While I was talking to the young mother, she fed the child from her breast and continued our conversation in the most natural manner. A month before, I would have been embarrassed, but I had been present at so many infant meals on the way down that I took it as a matter of course.

Our host decided that a rabbit should be killed in our honour, so his wife went out of the door where several tame black and white rabbits were nibbling the grass and seized the fattest she could find. She then brought it back into the parlour, wrung its neck, and skinned it with expert hands. The skin was then stretched on sticks and hung over the fireplace to dry. One of the daughters chopped up the still steaming carcase, which was then fried in olive oil and herbs.

Ten of us sat down to the best dinner I had tasted in Italy. Everything was perfectly cooked and the light red wine that was served with it was quite unlike anything I had ever tasted. Our host kept leaving the table to replenish the two large wine jugs, which were empty a few minutes after they appeared on the table. Everyone was in high spirits, and I think I spoke better Italian that evening than I ever shall again.

We sat round the table until quite late in the evening, drinking wine with our host while his wife washed and darned our socks. By the time we were led off to the cowshed for the night, we were feeling extremely merry and I think we both went to sleep as soon as we hit the hay.

We awoke the next morning with the feeling that we had dined too well the night before. Our host took us upstairs to the parlour and insisted on giving us more wine. We both had dry throats and, as there was no tea or coffee, we followed the principle that what killed you the night before will cure you in the morning. We were anxious to make an early start, but our host would not hear of it, as his daughter had been up since six thirty preparing a special dish of pasta for us. We were to be shown exactly how pasta should be cooked. The girl was in no hurry, and we watched her roll out the dough until it was as thin as paper. She then cut it into long, thin, narrow strips and put it in the pot to boil. Meanwhile, her mother had been preparing a special tomato sauce to put over it. It certainly looked and smelt most appetizing.

While we were waiting for our breakfast, our host and one of his sons wrote letters to the eldest son, who was a prisoner of war in Australia. They gave me the letters to post in Naples; I put them in the notebook that contained my second attempt at this story.

The pasta was ready at last and we each sat down to a large bowl filled to the brim with this *specialità della casa*. Our host produced more wine, and insisted on filling our glasses at every conceivable opportunity. It was the largest and best breakfast that I have ever eaten, and when I got up to say goodbye I felt I could walk to Naples and back in a day. It took some time to say goodbye to this large family, whose liberal hospitality was destined to be the last we were to enjoy on our journey.

We pushed off down the hill and made for the mountains above Gubbio. We were both in excellent spirits, and to begin with everything seemed to go right for us. We found a path running along the side of the mountain, which saved us going up and down the usual deep ravines. The plain lay to our right, criss-crossed by vineyards and small streams. As far as we could see, there were no roads running across the plain, the main road to Gubbio being parallel with the mountainside.

We were soon faced with a difficult decision. Our path came to an abrupt end and we were forced to descend a precipitous side of the hill and climb up the equally steep slope the other side. We arrived somewhat exhausted at a small house, where we asked the way. The woman inside appeared nervous and incredibly stupid; we could get no sense out of her. Gubbio was about a mile in front of us, tucked in the side of the mountain. We had either to cross the plain this side of Gubbio or to climb above the town and continue another ten miles to a spot where the plain ended in a narrow neck. Whatever happened, we had to get to the mountains on the other side of the plain between Gubbio and Perugia.

If we had been faced with this decision in the early part of our trip, we should most certainly have chosen the longer and safer route. But after walking unhindered for a month we were getting careless, and our somewhat unusual breakfast made us disregard any possible danger. We both felt lazy, so we decided to cross the plain on our side of the town.

We walked down to the main road and were unwise enough to ask for a drink at a shop by the road. The owner refused to supply us, so we crossed the road and started to walk over the fields of the plain. The ground was very muddy and the going was not improved by numerous deep ditches full of water. By the time we had crossed the plain we were very weary, and we did not relish the prospect of climbing the mountains on the other side. We made for a small village to our left, and followed a by-road running parallel with the plain we had just crossed. It was a great relief to walk on a road after the mud of the plain.

We had just passed by a farmhouse when the first danger signal appeared. A civilian on a motorcycle passed slowly by, regarding us with obvious interest. In normal times, a middle aged civilian on a motorcycle can scarcely be a cause for worry. But in December 1943 no Italian civilian was allowed any petrol by the Germans. It was therefore most probable that this man was connected, in one way or another, with the Fascists. I mentioned this fact to Ronald, and he agreed that the appearance of a civilian motorcyclist was sinister. However, he had gone on and we did not worry.

We reached the village and asked the way to Monte Luiano, a small village in the mountains. We were directed up a mule track and were just starting off again when a woman came up to us and pointed out that much the easiest way was to follow the by-road, which would take us up into the mountains half a mile further on.

Whether this woman was a spy, I do not know. The Germans were at that time offering three thousand lire to anyone who captured a British officer, but our faith in the *contadini* was such that this bribe did not worry us. The breakfast was having its effect; to go by road was much pleasanter than climbing mountains, so off we went down the road.

Bacchus must be a Fascist!

We noticed that the people we passed were nervous when we talked to them, and we came to our senses at last when the man on the motorcycle passed us for a second time. But the turning point up the mountain was only a little way ahead, so we hurried on. Just

114

before we reached the turning, a sinister-looking man wearing a black overcoat and black felt hat came walking towards us. As we passed him, he asked us where we were going, and I in turn asked him the way to Monte Luiano. He tried to appear friendly, but told us to keep left towards Gubbio. We knew this was wrong, so we hurried on to the turning up the hill, at which point the road branched left to Gubbio.

I remarked to Ronald that the black-coated gentleman seemed very much the cloak and dagger type, and that the sooner we got into the hills the better. We hurried on as fast as we could, but when we looked round we saw the man in black following us at a distance of two hundred yards. We increased our pace and he increased his. It was obvious that we were being followed. As there was no cover on either side of the road, we thought it best to hurry on up the mountain until we reached some cover where we could leave the road for good. We walked faster and faster, but the black figure kept up with us.

Suddenly, we heard the noise of a motorcycle coming from the direction of Gubbio. The noise came nearer and nearer, and eventually we saw the motorcycle, followed by a car, appear round a corner at the bottom of the hill. We realized at once that the motorcyclist had fetched the Fascist militia from Gubbio, while the other man kept us in sight.

I shouted to Ronald, 'Fascists, we must make a dash for it!' and we ran off across the fields on our left as fast as we could go.

The mud stuck to our boots and the faster we tried to run, the heavier our feet became. The man following us saw us go and he started to shout and wave his arms.

I was carrying a mackintosh, a blanket-roll and a haversack. It was neck or nothing, and I realized that all ballast must be thrown overboard at once. The mackintosh was the first to go, then the blanket roll. I was just about to jettison the haversack when I remembered the letters inside my book. If they were found the *contadini* would be for it. I decided to hold on to the haversack until I could find a bush to hide it in.

By this time, the militia had left their car and were in full cry across the fields, much to the astonishment of a young boy working a plough. For the first time in my life, I realized what it must be like to be a hunted fox, and for the next few minutes I became positively anti-blood sports.

We were going fairly well, though the pace was beginning to tell, when we were confronted by an obstacle which made Becher's Brook seem like a small ditch. A small but deep ravine yawned in front of us. The sides and bottom were thickly covered with brambles, but there was no way round, so we dived down the side, crashing through the undergrowth like a hunter taking on a thick 'bullfinch'. The opposite bank was impossibly steep, and after two frantic attempts it was obvious that we could not climb it in time. The only hope was to hide. I hid the haversack under a thick bush, and concealed myself as best I could among the undergrowth.

The militia reached the ravine and immediately lined the near bank. From this position they could observe any attempt we might make to get up the other side. They were shouting with excitement and started yelling instructions to each other. Then the trouble started with a vengeance.

They began to fire into the undergrowth. There is nothing that a Fascist soldier likes more than shooting at people who cannot shoot back, and at that moment I felt sure that our last hour had come. The bullets came nearer our particular piece of cover, so we rather naturally decided that our only hope was to surrender. I gave Ronald a push and told him to put his hands up. He stood up, and as he raised his hands a Fascist lieutenant aimed his rifle at him and pulled the trigger. Ronald must have had a premonition that this was going to happen as a split second before the officer pulled the trigger he fell over backwards. I heard the bullet and naturally thought that Ronald had been shot through the head. The prospect of surrender now appeared very unattractive. My fears were short-lived, as Ronald scrambled up and shouted to the Italian to hold his fire. This seemed the right moment for me to put in an appearance, so I came out from behind the bush with my hands in the air.

There were six members of the militia facing us – all of them officers. They were all shouting and pointing rifles or revolvers at us, with their fingers stroking the triggers. They shouted to us to keep our hands above our heads and to come out of the ravine. It was no easy job to walk up the steep bank with one's hands in the air, but if we made any attempt to lower our hands the militia officers shouted louder and their fingers moved on their triggers.

Ronald managed to get out, but I became caught by an obstinate bramble bush entwined round my middle. I was quite unable to move, and shouted to the Italians that I was stuck, but they shouted back to me to come out. It was a complete deadlock. I pushed and shoved and the Italians shouted, but the brambles held me as tight as the tar baby held the fox in the story of Brer Rabbit. Eventually, with a terrific heave, I freed myself from the brambles and fell flat on my face. I expected another burst from the lieutenant's rifle but he only shouted 'Out! Out!' I picked myself up and reached the top of the ravine in safety.

We were marched across the field to the car with our hands in the air. The militia officers continued to shout, and for some unknown reason they arrested the unfortunate boy who was standing by his plough.

When we reached the car, the motorcyclist and his accomplice were standing there holding revolvers. They seemed delighted with their day's work, which had netted them three thousand lire apiece. It was not until we had been thoroughly searched that we were allowed to lower our hands. The ploughboy was in tears, and his parents were standing by wringing their hands. I told the militia officers that we had never seen the boy before, and he was then released.

A more ridiculous collection of men than the six militia officers it would be hard to imagine. One of them had an English Tommy gun which he said he had captured off a parachutist the week before. I told him that the gun would not be much use to him as it had not got a magazine. He seemed very surprised at this, and not a little disappointed.

We were then bundled into the car, and with two Italians standing on the running board they drove us off in triumph to Gubbio.

Our walk south was over. It had lasted thirty-three days, twenty-six of which were spent walking. We had covered some four hundred miles. We had done quite well, but not well enough.

7

Perugia

We were taken straight to the Fascist militia barracks in Gubbio, where we were subjected to a further search and questioned by the officer in charge. I had lost all my belongings with the exception of the blanket Giacomo had given me. I had on me a small diary, but the names of Italians who had helped us were written in code. As soon as we reached the barracks the Italian officers calmed down and treated us quite well. They asked us to give them the names of the *contadini* who had helped us on our journey south, but did not seem very surprised when we refused. We were then taken off to the kitchen and given a good meal.

The militia force in Gubbio consisted entirely of boys between the ages of sixteen and nineteen, who hardly knew how to hold a rifle, let alone fire one. They were very sorry for us, and told us that they had been forced into the militia because their parents were imprisoned if they did not join up. Several of them had tried to escape service but had had to return to free their parents. Many of them were university students. They were paid twelve lire a day, plus a daily allowance of twenty cigarettes and two meals, with as much bread as they wanted. As far as we could see, the militia boys did absolutely nothing all day except eat. They told us that when they marched around the town they were liable to be shot at by anti-Fascists, and we did see one boy who had just returned from hospital with a wound in his leg.

The officers made a great fuss of the boys. Their methods of discipline were most odd, for instead of reproving them in the usual military manner they would pull their noses or gently smack their faces. Despite this somewhat unusual behaviour, the boys seemed frightened of the officers, whose only duty seemed to be the supervision of meals. Before any meal there would be at least four officers in the kitchen all giving different advice to a rather harrassed cook.

We spent the rest of the day in the kitchen because it was the only warm place in the building. The major in charge of the barracks informed us that he was full of humanitarian spirit and would not handcuff us as he should do. I don't know where he got this strange idea from.

In the evening we were taken down a long passage and locked in a room with another smaller room leading out of it. The windows were barred and there was no furniture of any sort in either room. In one corner there was a small wooden platform covered with straw, which we were told was our bed. The room stank and the straw was damp. The previous inmates of the room had scrawled on the wall in Italian, 'Abandon hope all ye who enter here', so it was hardly surprising that we were both very depressed.

We were given two blankets each and told to settle down for the night, but we were not allowed to turn out the light. The guard slept next door and was able to watch our movements through a little hole in the wall; we could hear a sentry walking up and down outside the window. An extremely uncomfortable night was not improved by the guards visiting us every two hours. Ronald was violently sick during the night.

The next morning we were taken off to the kitchen, where we remained until after lunch. We were given as many cigarettes as we wanted and more food than we could possibly eat. The orderly officer told us that we would be leaving early next morning for Perugia, where we would be handed over to the German authorities.

After lunch we went back to our cell and lay in the straw. Two of the boys came in and asked if we would like to see a pretty girl. This seemed an attractive proposal and the boys told us to come into the smaller room. Two girls were peering through the small barred window. They had climbed up the outside wall and were hanging on by the bars. We talked to the girls for a while and then one went off to fetch her mother. After a few minutes there was much pushing and shoving outside the window, and then an old woman's face appeared at the bars. Our conversation was interrupted by the sounds of an officer coming down the passage, whereupon the girls released their hold on the bars and slid to the ground, leaving the old lady clinging perilously to the window. She eventually let go and, judging by the noise, fell in a heap on the street outside.

While we had been talking to the women, I noticed a brick missing from the wall. On further investigation I discovered that other bricks could be removed without difficulty. It would be easy to escape if we could pick the right moment. We decided to work on the bricks that night after the orderly officer and guard had made their midnight rounds of inspection. The prospects appeared very bright.

We went back to the kitchen for tea and stayed there until it was time to go to bed. The hours seemed to drag by as I sat thinking about our chances of escape. One of the boys asked me what I was thinking about and I told him that I was memorizing the faces of the two spies in order that I could come back after the war and cut their throats. He seemed to think this a great joke and I only hope that he notified the spies of my intention.

Bedtime arrived at last, and we went off to our cell. We arranged that when the officer had been round I would work on the wall and Ronald would stay in bed and pretend to carry on a conversation with me so that the sentries would think I was still in the room.

The officer came on his rounds earlier than usual, and just as he was leaving the other room he switched his torch on the wall and discovered the loose brick. The game was up. He posted another sentry in the narrow street outside the window and our last hope of escape evaporated.

We were awakened at four in the morning by the orderly officer, who told us to get up as the train for Perugia left at a quarter to six. We were given a good breakfast in the kitchen before setting off on foot for the station. It was pitch dark as we walked through the streets of Gubbio with the officer and three guards. The guards carried their rifles at the ready, and the officer had his hand on his revolver. It would have been suicidal to make a bolt for it, and at that hour of the morning my courage was not very high.

The railway from Gubbio to Perugia was a single-track line that ran level with the main road round the mountains. Our journey was expected to last three hours. There was a large crowd at the station by the time an ancient engine, drawing four rickety old carriages, arrived in at six o'clock. There was the usual scramble for seats, and when everyone was squeezed in we got into a carriage and turned six civilians out of their seats. They looked daggers at the guards, but seeing the Fascist uniform they kept quiet.

We had to change trains twice. The last train had to climb a steep incline to reach the old city of Perugia, which is perched on top of a hill.

We were marched through the busy streets to what I imagine were the municipal buildings. Here we were interviewed by a fat and bored civilian who had an Italian lieutenant with him as interpreter. The officer had recently been repatriated from Africa on the grounds of ill health. He seemed quite sympathetic and gave us the impression that he was rather ashamed of being a Fascist.

We were once again asked the names of the *contadini* who had helped us and how we had got our civilian clothes. Our answer was the same as before. We were then asked when we thought the war would end, and we expressed the opinion that a few months would see the end of Italy. The civilian sighed and said that he hoped we were right.

Several telephone calls were put through while we were in the room. There was much talk of the German authorities, so we naturally presumed that we were to be handed over to the Germans that day. After waiting in the building for over an hour, we were driven away in a car to an enormous yellow building. As I got out of the car I looked up at the rows of little windows, and to my horror saw that it was a civilian prison.

The large iron gates were opened by a warder and we found ourselves in the courtyard of the prison. My morale sank to my boots as we were led off to the prison office, where a surly warder wrote down our particulars and took away our money, watches and other possessions, which he locked in a drawer after giving us a receipt.

While we were in the office two prisoners came in wearing the brown and white striped dress of the Italian convict. For one ghastly moment I thought we were going to be dressed in these clothes. In a few minutes another warder arrived with a bunch of keys and told us to follow him.

The prison was built in a modern style, with four wings forming a star from the round central hall. We looked up from the ground floor at the four galleried floors above with their lines of locked cell doors. It reminded me of the American prison film, *The Big House.*

As we walked down the passage we passed door after door, each with its little peephole in the centre and the names of its inmates written on a card framed in the door. Eventually the warder stopped and opened one of the cell doors. Inside were four South African soldiers lying on straw mattresses and smoking cigarettes. By this time we were very angry and told the warder that the least he could do was to put us in a cell by ourselves. He scratched his head, slammed the cell door and took us further along the passage to an empty cell. We were pushed inside and the door locked behind us.

For nearly a minute we stood in the middle of the cell speechless with rage and mortification, before giving vent to our feelings with every conceivable oath that we could remember. This was really rock bottom! A cold cell in a civilian prison in Italy. This was how Fascists treated prisoners of war!

The cell was fifteen feet long, seven feet wide and about sixteen feet high. The walls were of whitewashed stone, with a small window high up at the top end, criss-crossed with thick iron bars. The only sanitary arrangements were a rusty tin concealed in a hole in the wall, accessible from the inside and outside of the cell. A convict emptied the tin at six in the morning and five in the evening.

Two convicts escorted by a warder brought us two board beds with filthy straw mattresses, and two very small blankets each. A tin basin and two aluminium eating bowls were put on the shelf, and the warder and convicts then withdrew. Our razors had been taken from us in case we tried to cut our throats – perhaps it was just as well!

We sat down on our beds feeling dejected, desperate and extremely cold. We were completely helpless in a foreign gaol and as far as we knew we might stay there until the end of the war. It is strictly against the Geneva Convention to keep prisoners of war in a civilian gaol, and we determined at the first opportunity to demand to see the governor, the head warder, a priest or anyone else who might help us.

Soon after midday the door was opened, and a convict told us to bring our bowls out into the passage and get our meal. We stood in a queue of convicts while another convict filled our bowls with a thick vegetable soup and gave us each a loaf of bread. Before we returned to our cell we had an opportunity to look at our fellow sufferers. Some were in civilian clothes and others were in the regulation striped dress of the convict. They were all immensely interested in us and swarmed around asking a multitude of questions. Before we could answer, we were ordered back to our cell and the door slammed once more – but not before we had put in a request to see the head warder.

The soup was moderately good and the bread very fresh, but it came as a shock to learn that this was the only meal we would have each day. We were, however, told that there was a prison canteen from which, provided we had money, we could buy a few cigarettes, some cheap wine and tins of anchovies at an exorbitant price.

Later that afternoon the governor, or as he is known in Italy the inspector, of the prison came to see us. He was dressed in civilian clothes and wore a scarlet tie. The first thing that struck one was his large hooked nose. He asked me if I would prefer him to speak in French, and when I agreed to this he had the impertinence to ask me if everything was all right. I was so angry that I could not find the words in French to express my feelings. I can't remember what I said, but the gist of my remarks was that it was a disgrace to treat British officers in this way, that it was against the Geneva Convention, and what was he going to do about it. He was maddeningly calm and simply shrugged his shoulders, saying that it was not his fault, and that in any case we would only be detained for a few days. He then left us.

The next morning we were let out for an hour to exercise. The exercise yard consisted of a series of outdoor compartments constructed like the run to a dog kennel, and separated from each other by a high wall. We felt, and no doubt looked, ridiculous as we paced up and down this small enclosure, but it was a relief to get out of the cell for an hour. Before returning, I asked the sergeant warder if we could see a priest, but he could promise nothing definite.

Later that morning the air raid alarm was sounded. All the cell doors were unlocked, and we were allowed to walk up and down the passage. We were immediately surrounded by a crowd of fellow prisoners who were extremely sympathetic and did their best to cheer us up. One day in prison had banished any self-respect that we had left; we had to live with convicts, so why not fraternize with them?

They were a remarkable collection. Some of them were mere boys serving sentences for black market activities and other anti-Fascist offences. In many cases the prisoners did not know how long they were in for, but they did not appear to care, and were confident of release when the British arrived. Their families were permitted to send them food and wine each day, and I think they were allowed to write letters. One boy admitted to us that he had been connected with every type of black market racket. He had been tried by a special tribunal in Rome and sentenced to twenty-seven years' imprisonment. Many of the political prisoners had been released when Badoglio came to power, but had been locked up again when the Germans took over.

One of the strangest men was an Argentine anarchist with a flaming red beard, who attached himself to us at every available opportunity. He appeared to be a man of good breeding and had a very good, if somewhat warped, brain. He spoke excellent French and was most anxious to learn English. Whenever the sirens sounded he would come to our cell and ask for a list of English words to learn. The last ten years of his life had almost all been spent in prison. He had very definite views about life and could not keep his mouth shut, with the result that he was constantly making trouble. 'If a man has views of his own,' he said, 'he should express them, even if it means he is put in prison.' He had no idea how long he was in for, but unless he changed his ideas I imagine he spent the rest of his life in gaol.

The old lags made one feel rather sad. Most of them had grey hair and grey faces, with purple shadows under their eyes. Their expression was one of resignation, as if life for them was finished. One of them, who ran the prison canteen accounts, visited us quite often. He had murdered his wife and was serving a seventeen-year sentence, of which he had just completed twelve. He seemed a very good fellow and perhaps his wife deserved her fate. He was not the only murderer in the prison, but the others did not look very attractive so we did not make their acquaintance.

On the second day one of the more pleasant warders took us along to the room where prisoners were allowed to write letters. There we met three university professors who had been locked up for teaching anti-Fascist doctrines. They promised to try to get information through to the Red Cross that we were in prison, but nothing came of it.

When we had been in prison two days a civilian arrived, and took us off in a car to be interviewed by the Fascist commandant of Perugia. We entered an impressive looking building and, having been ushered through three ante-rooms, found ourselves standing outside the great man's door. Everyone spoke in hushed voices, and by the fuss that was made, you would have thought that Mussolini himself was in the next room! A uniformed officer beckoned to us to enter the sanctuary.

The room was large and well furnished, with a thick Persian carpet covering the floor. The commandant sat at a desk on a raised dais with a shaded green spotlight focused on him from behind. At floor level, two other desks were occupied by Fascist officers, their chests smothered in decorations.

The act was certainly well staged, and I suppose it would have impressed an Italian. We stood in our filthy clothes in front of the commandant's desk, but he did not look up for several moments. He then sent for an interpreter.

The same questions were again asked us regarding the *contadini*, and we gave the same answers. I then asked the interpreter if I could ask the commandant a few questions. The request was granted, and once again we gave vent to our pent-up feelings.

Did the commandant think it was correct to lock British officers up with convicts? Did he know that he was acting contrary to the Geneva Convention? How long were we to be kept in prison? Could we buy food from a restaurant and have it sent in?

The commandant replied that he was quite aware that he was acting against the Geneva Convention, but the British had treated Italian prisoners in India so badly that he was getting his own back. That was that! He gave instructions that we should be allowed to buy food, and we were then dismissed from the room.

When we returned to the prison we saw the head warder, who promised to arrange for food to be sent in from a restaurant, but added that it might not appear for a day or two.

At exercise the next morning we were locked in with seven Yugoslavs and four British prisoners who had arrived the night before. Three of them were South Africans (including one of the batmen from Fontanellato), and the other a typical cockney 'Tommy'. They were a most amusing quartet and kept us entertained with their stories of the walk through Italy. They appeared to have had prodigious appetites, and on one occasion they had stolen a large turkey while passing a farm. By the time they reached the next farm they had plucked the bird, and asked the *contadini* to cook it for them. They assured us that the bird weighed fourteen pounds and that they had eaten it at one session.

The next day the promised food arrived, and life took on a much rosier complexion. After the welcome feast, we slept for the rest of the day.

The days passed incredibly slowly. With the exception of the daily air raid warning and the hour's exercise, we had nothing to do but sit in our cell and take turns to read Ronald's Bible, the only form of literature we possessed. Ronald read the *Acts of the Apostles*, while I sought inspiration from the *Book of Job*.

On Saturday 11 December, after we had been in prison five days, another officer from Fontanellato, Captain Hargreaves, arrived and was put in our cell. Hargreaves was a regular soldier with thirty years' service to his credit, and his disgust at finding himself in a civilian gaol knew no bounds. We were just beginning to get slightly acclimatized and did our best to cheer up poor

Hargreaves, who sat on his bed with his head in his hands in the lowest depths of depression. We ordered extra food and wine from the restaurant, which together with the canteen wine helped even Hargreaves to forget his troubles.

The days dragged by; each one seemed to go slower than the last. Worst of all, our money was beginning to run out; we had visions of having to exist once more on the prison diet.

Some of the warders were very good to us and did their best to make life more pleasant. There was one very unpleasant man who went out of his way to be rude and tiresome to us and to the thirty other British soldiers in the prison. The most irritating ritual carried out by the warders was the testing of the window bars in the morning and evening, when one of them would enter the cell with a convict carrying a ladder, climb up to the window and bang the bars with a small crowbar in order to make sure that they had not been sawn through. We could hear the banging all over the prison, morning and evening.

We asked constantly for a barber to shave us, but the answer was always '*domani*'. It was not until we had been in gaol ten days that we were given a shave by the prison barber, a convict who was serving a long sentence. I did not like to ask him what he was inside for, in case he should say that it was for cutting his wife's throat!

Soon after Hargreaves' arrival at the prison, a civilian from Florence was brought in to serve a sentence of unstated length for 'giving help to Englishmen and Jews'. The prisoner, a sallow-faced, middle-aged man, was well dressed and obviously fairly well off. I used to talk to him in the passage during the air raids, and he told me his story. He assured me that it was a case of mistaken identity, as he knew no Jews or Englishmen in Florence to whom he could be of any assistance; had he known any, he said, he would most certainly have helped them. The Fascist authorities took him before the German commandant, and he denied the allegations against him. He was promptly taken away by the Germans and beaten with rubber truncheons before being sent to Perugia gaol. He insisted on taking me to his cell and showing me his back, which was black and blue from the flogging he had received. A fine example of Nazi and Fascist justice.

The last of our money had gone by 20 December, and the head warder summoned us to his office. He was sitting at his desk with a broad smile on his face and asked us what we were going to do. He could not resist making the observation that the 'English milord' would soon have to tighten his belt. We were just considering what we could sell when the little man produced Ronald's watch out of a drawer and asked him how much he wanted for it. Watches in Italy were practically unobtainable at the time, and Ronald should have got a good price for it. Hargreaves and I, for purely selfish reasons, thought it would be an excellent idea for Ronald to sell his watch. I was quite safe, as my watch had already been stolen at Fontanellato. Ronald magnanimously agreed to the sale and started bargaining with the head warder, who immediately found fault with the watch and finally produced an expert jeweller out of a side door, like a conjurer pulls a white rabbit from a hat! It was now quite clear that the little *capo guardia* had had his eye on our accounts and Ronald's watch ever since we had been in prison. The jeweller examined the watch and found as many faults with it as an Irishman trying to buy a horse cheaply. The combination of the two Italians was too much for Ronald, and he agreed to let the watch go for six hundred lire. I am certain that the correct price was nearer fifteen hundred lire, but six hundred would keep us in food for nearly a week, and as far as Hargreaves and I were concerned that was highly satisfactory.

The next morning, our seventeenth day in gaol, we were told that the Germans had sent a truck for us and that we were to leave at once. We went along to the *capo guardia*'s office to be handed back our money and other belongings, and Ronald demanded his watch back in exchange for the six hundred lire. The *capo guardia* put on the most innocent expression and regretted that he had already sold it. Nice work!

There were thirty British and South African other ranks in the prison and they all assembled at the warder's office to reclaim their belongings. The situation was too much for the *capo guardia*, who got into a hopeless muddle with the various names and odd amounts of money. The German officer became more and more impatient, and the Italian more and more excited. It took nearly two hours to get the matter straightened out, and when we left the *capo guardia* was in a state of collapse.

We were marched through the prison gates and pushed into the back of a large open truck, with two Germans in the front and four Italian guards in the back. The German officer announced, before the truck started, that if anyone tried to escape he would shoot the lot of us. I suppose there is nothing like making oneself absolutely clear!

8

In German hands

The transit camp to which we were going lay twenty miles south of Perugia, about halfway between Assisi and Spoleto. As we drove along, we noticed a fair amount of damage caused by RAF raids on railway stations and bridges. The camp was situated on the side of a hill just outside the village of Pisciano, overlooking the Tiber valley.

When we arrived, a considerable number of prisoners were standing by the wire to welcome us, and I soon noticed several familiar faces from Fontanellato. Most of the officers were in ragged civilian clothes, and it was apparent that they had not visited a barber for several weeks. The camp was not very large; it consisted of several marquees and two or three wooden sheds, all of which were crowded with prisoners. The officers occupied the huts and the other ranks the marquees. It would have been difficult to imagine a stranger collection of men. There were Chinese, Yugoslavs, Frenchmen, Englishmen, Canadians, Americans, Italians, Greeks, Arabs, Russians, South Africans, Indians, Australians and New Zealanders. Some of them were prisoners recaptured from Italian prison camps; others had been captured recently on the Italian front; many, such as the Chinese, had been arrested in Italy for not holding identity papers.

It was an appallingly squalid place, which made even Capua seem like a paradise. All the prisoners were crawling with lice, the food was filthy, and the sanitation hopelessly inadequate. The hut in which I lived was fifty-two feet long and sixteen feet wide, and contained forty-eight officers sleeping on double decker wooden beds. With the exception of a narrow central aisle running between the sets of beds and a small space in front of the two small stoves, there was nowhere to stand in the room. When we arrived there were not enough beds to go round, and I had to sleep on the floor. Luckily the only floor space was in front of the stove, so I spent the night in comparative warmth.

The German guards were a far better type of soldier than we found in the permanent camps in Germany, and the commandant, an Austrian, was quite agreeable. He had managed to secure some

Red Cross parcels, which were issued to prisoners on arrival. The German officer, who acted as interpreter, had been taken prisoner by the British in the desert, but had managed to escape through Turkey.

A rather unfortunate state of affairs existed in the camp when we arrived. The senior major in the camp (there were no colonels) happened to be an Indian officer, and he took over the job of SBO. He could not have been nicer, and with the exception of his colour, he was completely English in every way. He had been educated at Eton and had spent most of his life in England. The English officers in the camp were only too pleased to have him as SBO, but the Germans considered it an outrageous appointment and refused to cooperate with him in any way. They went out of their way to insult him on every occasion, and refused to grant any concession he asked for. On one occasion he was standing in front of the parade during roll call and a German NCO deliberately pushed him to one side, telling him that he should get out of the way when a German soldier passed. The situation went from bad to worse, but was finally relieved when some other senior majors arrived at the camp shortly before we left.

I had not been in the camp a day before I was covered in lice. There was nothing to do about it, as there were no delousing baths. Every night, just before going to bed, we took off our clothes and had a lice hunt. It was quite funny to hear the shouts of triumph when a particularly large louse was run to ground.

We spent a lot of the day listening to and comparing accounts of our adventures since leaving Fontanellato. Many officers had got as far south as the river Sangro, only to be recaptured when in sight of the British lines. Many had suffered from exposure crossing the snow-covered mountains, and we heard reports of others who had been killed in the minefields. One officer, John Measures, had had particularly bad luck. He and his three companions had walked into a minefield when approaching the British lines. Measures escaped injury, but his companions were badly injured, one of them having an eye blown out. Measures had to get assistance for the wounded, and the only way he could achieve that was to go back and ask the Germans to help him. He soon found a German outpost, and the soldiers there even sympathized with him in his bad luck, as they told him that there were no Germans between him and the British lines.

Another batch of officers, who had left Pisciano just before we arrived, were bombed by the RAF in their train on the way to Germany. Many of them managed to escape once more in the ensuing chaos. Dermot Chichester, who had been with us in Fontanellato, was among this party. He managed to hide up in the Rome district and got back to England in June 1944.

A great tragedy occurred at Acquilla during the bombing of the railway yard by Allied planes. A party of some two hundred British men had been herded into wired-in cattle trucks for transport to Germany. Their train was standing alongside a German ammunition train in Acquilla station when a formation of Allied bombers arrived on the scene. The target was the ammunition train and the bombing was dead accurate. The ammunition train went up in a terrific explosion, blowing many of the adjacent cattle trucks to pieces. A number of German soldiers were also killed.

One of the most daring escapes from a prison camp took place while we were at Pisciano. The camp was surrounded by the usual wire, with elevated sentry platforms at each corner. The sentries all had miniature searchlights which they played up and down the wire during the night. The camp was on the side of a hill; it was noticed that when the lights were directed up the wire fence facing the guard room, there was a narrow trough of ground which always remained in shadow, no matter which light was flashing up and down. Four officers decided to crawl along this trough of ground, which was no more than two feet wide, cut the wire and crawl down the shadow to freedom. The shadow passed directly by the German guard room, which made the attempt even more perilous. In addition, the sentries were constantly walking up and down the wire, so the effort would have to be timed to take place when the sentries had passed that particular spot. If the officers were discovered, by either the sentry on patrol or one on the platform, there was not the slightest doubt that they would be fired on and killed.

Lots were drawn to decide who should crawl out first, cut the wire, and then return for the other three. The chosen man crawled along the shadow and lay on his stomach facing the wire; the sentry passed and noticed nothing, so he started to snip the fence. It is extremely difficult to cut taut wire without making a noise, and on this occasion the sentry heard a slight click. He called up to the man on the platform, who immediately switched his light up the wire, but thanks to the shadow saw nothing. When he had cut a small opening the daring escapee crawled back to his companions, and all four of them then returned up the shadow to the opening to await their moment. Everything went according to plan, and they made their escape under the very noses of the Germans in the guard room. It was a splendid effort that required cool nerves and infinite courage. When the Germans discovered the escape the next morning they were furious, and took their revenge on the remaining prisoners by making us stand up outside the wire in fours for three hours while they searched the huts for tools that might be used for escape.

Our Indian SBO asked the Germans for a little wine and cigarettes to brighten up our Christmas Day. The request met with no response beyond a wooden box full of very sticky raisins and the usual ration of potato soup. It was the dullest Christmas I have ever spent, even worse than the previous one in Tunis hospital. In the evening, the German interpreter came into the hut and made a little speech in which he regretted that we had to spend Christmas under such depressing conditions and wished us the compliments of the season.

Several other officers had arrived from Acquilla on Christmas Eve, and the Germans announced that as the camp was now full we would shortly be leaving for Germany. We looked forward to leaving Pisciano, but we hardly relished the prospect of a train journey through Italy with RAF planes chasing the trains.

We left on 27 December. Our party consisting of about seventy-five officers and a thousand other ranks. We were all subjected to the most thorough search before leaving, and we did not leave for the station until three o'clock. Despite the search, quite a few tools were smuggled out of the camp, so there was still a chance of breaking out of the train.

When we reached the station we found the usual cattle trucks awaiting our arrival. The windows and doors were wired up and there was a little straw on the floor. Forty officers were jammed into each truck, and the doors were bolted and wired. No sentries travelled in the trucks with us, but trucks full of German soldiers were placed at intervals along the train. Each officer was given a piece of Würst sausage and some bread before leaving on a journey that we were told might take anything from two to five days. As there were no Germans in the trucks with us, there was a good chance of cutting our way out before we crossed the Brenner.

The truck I was in contained French, Italian, Yugoslav, Greek and British officers. John Measures, who had had such bad luck in his attempt to get through the lines, was among our party, and had managed to smuggle in a knife and a piece of iron with which it would be possible to make a hole in the side of the truck.

We were extremely uncomfortable, the thin covering of straw on the floor being quite inadequate. It was also very cold. We decided to wait until it was dark before getting to work on the walls. The Germans were fully alert to the possibility of escape, and once darkness fell they started to fire their rifles off up and down the train whenever it slowed, stopped or moved on again. This was a clever idea and definitely made one realize that escape was going to be no easy matter. When the train stopped for more than a minute, the soldiers got out and patrolled up and down the line. The only hope was to cut a panel and burst it open just as the train was starting after a stop. We estimated that at least eight of us could jump through the hole before the train gathered speed. The German bullets were only being fired at random, and we would be unlikely to stop one.

John Measures, an Italian naval officer and a Yugoslav worked like slaves as soon as it was dark, and by two in the morning the panel was ready. Those who wanted to escape were told to stand by to jump after the next stop. I arranged to go with a French officer. It was an exciting moment as the eight of us stood up in the truck waiting for the next stop. We worked out that the train was now north of Florence, a suitable place to jump ship.

The train came to a halt and we waited in deathly silence for it to move on again. The Germans were firing their usual number of rounds and we hoped that the stop would not be a long one. Suddenly, we heard a patrol walking down the line.

Luck was against us once more. A German soldier flashed a lantern at the side of the truck and noticed the cut panel. He immediately shouted for an NCO, who came running down the line from another carriage. The door of the truck was opened and the Germans climbed into the carriage shouting at the tops of their voices.

They made everyone in the carriage stand up and asked who had cut the panel. The young Italian naval officer showed splendid spirit and calmly announced that he had cut it, but we insisted that we had all had a hand in the job. The German NCO became very excited and said he would shoot everyone if anyone tried to escape. He also demanded the tools we had worked with. There was no point in trying to hide them, so we gave them up. The NCO then calmed down and told us that if he had been a prisoner in England he would have done the same thing.

While the Germans were nailing up the panel we were all made to take our boots off. The Germans put them in a sack and took them away to their carriage; this put an end to any further attempt at escape. The train rolled on to the music of German rifle shots.

The rest of our journey was as uneventful as it was uncomfortable. We were given food and hot drinks at various halts and we reached the station of Moosberg in Bavaria at five o'clock on the evening of 30 December, having been in the train for three days and two nights. The RAF had left us in peace.

It was bitterly cold and snowing lightly when we lined up in the goods yard before marching off to the camp. The civilians must have thought us an odd assortment as we marched away. Hardly any of us were in uniform, and the civilian clothes most of us wore were in rags.

The camp was only half a mile from the railway station and we reached the main gates just before dusk. A more depressing-looking place it would be hard to imagine. The camp, a very large one, had existed during the First World War. Seventy thousand French prisoners had been sent to Moosberg after Dunkirk, and many of them were still there when we arrived. Accommodation consisted solely of long, low, wooden huts with a wide main street running down the centre. Facing the entrance gates was a square wooden tower adorned with a frieze depicting wounded and dejected Allied soldiers, under which were written the words TO BERLIN. Rather bad taste, even for a German.

In addition to the French soldiers there were a thousand or so Russians, Yugoslavs, Greeks and a few Italians. The most unusual members of the camp were a party of Yugoslav women partisans. They were the toughest looking women I have ever seen, and even the Germans seemed to have quite a respect for them. We had a chance to talk with them before we left, and they told us that the Germans were treating them well.

As soon as we arrived in the camp we were taken off to one of the huts and subjected to the usual search, always a very tedious performance. We were then taken to the clothing store, where we had to give up our civilian clothes in exchange for a varied assortment of uniforms. The Germans had collected a large quantity of foreign uniforms from the countries they had invaded, and these uniforms were distributed to incoming prisoners from Italy. By the time we were clothed we presented an even more grotesque appearance than before: some of us were in the light blue uniform of the French, others in the bright green of the Poles, the grey Czech or Yugoslav military dress; very few of the uniforms fitted, and some officers had a Polish tunic, French trousers, and Yugoslav hat. I was quite unable to find a pair of trousers big enough, so I was allowed to keep my dyed battledress ones. I was fortunate enough to get a grey double-breasted tunic that had once belonged to a Serbian major, and was warm and comfortable.

When we had all been kitted out, we marched down the main street of the camp to our quarters. Our hut lay at the bottom end of the camp, and by the time we arrived there we were covered in snow. The huts at Moosberg were separated from each other by barbed wire fencing, leaving just enough room for exercise round the building. Each hut was divided into two living rooms, with a small washhouse in the centre. When we entered our hut we found a large number of English prisoners already there, many of them from Fontanellato, and I soon saw several familiar faces.

The scene inside was one of indescribable chaos. The Germans had not prepared for our arrival; there were not enough beds to go round in what was already a very crowded hut. The beds were of the three-tier variety, arranged in blocks of twelve. The Germans assured us that there would be enough beds the next day but that we must do the best we could for that night.

The atmosphere was terrible – hardly surprising when one considers that there were one hundred and twenty-five officers sleeping, eating and smoking in such a small space. If a window was opened the occupants of nearby beds were practically frozen to death, so the windows remained tightly shut.

The other half of the hut, beyond the washhouse, was similarly small, and contained mostly officers who had recently been captured at Léros. They had spent fourteen days in cattle trucks between Athens and Moosberg. The day after my arrival I moved into this half of the hut with Jerry Saunders and Gussie Pearce from Fontanellato. It was just as crowded and uncomfortable. I managed to get a top tier bunk in the hope that any fresh air might rise to the ceiling.

The morning after our arrival we were marched off to a delousing station, where our bodies, clothes and bedding were completely freed from lice. It was a great relief to be able to lie in bed without scratching every few minutes.

While we were in the drying-off room of the delousing centre, which is similar to a Turkish bath, we saw several Russian prisoners undergoing the same treatment as ourselves. Several of them had been shaved with the formidable electric clippers we had noticed on our way from the showers. These clippers, which were used to rout lice from the more inaccessible parts of the body, had luckily not been required in our case. The Russians were a pathetic sight; they were so thin that the skin hung in loose folds from their bones. The Germans gave them the minimum amount to eat and they all slept together in a long hut with no mattresses, pillows or blankets. The only comforts supplied were wooden shavings to act as bedding. Their sufferings must have been appalling in the cold weather we were experiencing at the time.

When we returned to our hut we found a crowd of Russian prisoners putting up more three-tier beds for us. Most of them were dressed in old Polish uniforms, but several retained the Russian headdress of fur-lined cap. They had no proper boots, but had been given thick wooden clogs that they stuffed with straw. Many of the Russians were boys of thirteen and fourteen who had been captured with partisan groups. The German sentries did not treat them badly and seemed to regard them as a rather unfortunate crowd of animals. It was impossible to carry on a conversation with them, as they spoke only Russian. They made signs that they wanted cigarettes and food, and during the time they worked in the hut they received considerable quantities of both from our Red Cross parcels. Hot potatoes or soup were brought to us in large tin containers, and when these were emptied they were put outside, whereupon the Russians working in or around the hut would wipe round the sides in search of any leftovers. It was a tragic sight, and made us feel that we should have done more for them. We were told that Stalin did not recognize Russian prisoners and that nothing was done for them.

In one camp, where there were two thousand Russians, there was an outbreak of typhoid. The German medical authorities refused to do anything for them, and sixteen hundred of them died before a South African medical officer arrived on the scene and saved the remainder. When the Russians arrived at Moosberg several of them were so weak that they died under the showers of the delousing station. Another batch of prisoners was taken round Germany and exhibited like animals to the populace.

The Germans kept a number of Alsatian dogs, which they used

to patrol the wire at night and to keep the Russians in order. The dogs were splendidly trained, each with its own handler. They were fierce-looking creatures, and I would have hated to meet one in the dark. The Germans used these dogs at all their prison camps, and there is no doubt that they were very effective.

In one of the huts the Russians used to walk round the wire after lights out, so the Germans threatened to set the dogs on them. As the Russians paid no attention to this threat, two of the dogs were let loose inside the wire after dark. The next morning there were two Alsatian skins hanging on the wire, and the Russians had meat in their stew for lunch.

A very wide black market existed at Moosberg, thanks to the efforts of the French, who were able to bribe the Germans to do practically anything for cigarettes. It was for most of us the first sign of weakening in the discipline and morale of the German soldiers, which gradually increased as we moved from camp to camp.

A strange system existed among the French medical staff: they could take a holiday from captivity provided they could get someone from France to take their place. Many of the French went away and returned after six months. As a result of these changes we were able to hear many stories about the organization of the underground movement in France. The French prisoners also managed to fix up a wireless set on which they listened to BBC broadcasts. A résumé of these broadcasts was sent into our hut each day.

The only redeeming feature of Moosberg, with its snow outside and fug inside, were the walks that took place nearly every day. It was not difficult to get on these outings, as a great many officers refused to give their word not to try and escape.

The Germans, unlike the Italians, trusted a British officer when he gave his word, with the result that fifty of us were allowed out on walks with one German officer and a soldier to show us the way. We were not made to march in formation once we had left the prison gates but walked along as we pleased. It was always bitterly cold, but we soon warmed up when walking and returned to the huts feeling strong enough to face another twelve hours of squalor.

We did our best to make New Year's Eve a little brighter than the other dreary evenings by sitting up and drinking very light beer until midnight. At the stroke of midnight an accordion was produced and 'Auld Lang Syne' was sung in the appropriate manner. The evening was not a great success – the only effect it had on most of us was to keep us walking to and from the lavatory most of the night, a tiresome pastime.

The short period at Moosberg did much to promote good feeling between the British and the American officers. Many people who in peacetime would not have had the time or the desire really to learn about the American outlook on life, took the opportunity of doing so at Moosberg, and there is no doubt that many false impressions were removed.

A considerable number of British officers recaptured in Italy had passed through Moosberg before we arrived, and we were told that they had been sent to a permanent camp in Czechoslovakia. By 18 January the huts allotted to us were crammed full, and there were rumours of a move.

The first people to go were the RAF officers, who were sent to the special RAF camp. They were followed by the Greek and Yugoslav officers. On 20 January the American officers left for another camp, and one hundred and ninety of us were warned to be ready to depart the following day. The officers recently captured at Léros were to stay on at Moosberg, but the old hands were going to a camp in Czechoslovakia.

I dreaded the journey, but anything was preferable to remaining at Moosberg. I had felt unwell the entire time I was there, and the atmosphere of the place depressed me more than any other camp I had been to.

We left the hut at eight-thirty on the morning of 21 January and marched to another hut where we were to be searched, the most irritating part of any move. The Germans told us that our train would not be leaving until the afternoon and that orderlies were bringing some food to the searching hut. We queued up yet again for the usual thick potato soup and bread. After the meal we walked around the square to pass the time and to keep ourselves warm.

The German captain then suggested that the British officers should make a collection of cigarettes for their less fortunate allies. This proposal was readily agreed to, despite the protests of the four German guards who had the job of keeping the Russians in order during the sharing out of the cigarettes. Two blankets were laid on the ground, and we were invited to throw into them any cigarettes we wished to give to the Russians. In a few minutes over two thousand cigarettes had been donated. The job of dividing them up was taken on by Tony Watson, Crump Colbeck and Bill Lewis.

Watson and Crump were the comedians of the party and were both wearing the dark blue and red cap of the French *gendarme*. Bill Lewis was very tall, with a lock of fair hair hanging permanently over his forehead. They looked a funny trio as they knelt on the blankets to divide the cigarettes into batches of a hundred. The Russians were told to divide up into parties of ten, and a representative from each party was to fetch one hundred cigarettes from tobacconists Watson, Crump and Lewis.

The Russians eventually sorted themselves into tens and filed by the blanket to receive their cigarettes. For a moment it seemed as if everything would go according to plan, but when they had all filed past there were still several hundred cigarettes left over. Watson, Crump and Lewis once more knelt on the blanket and started to divide the cigarettes into smaller batches. But once the Russians had smelt an English cigarette their appetites were whetted and they began to lose control, despite the efforts of the dog and three sentries. Eventually, the inevitable occurred – a sudden scurry, a shout and the three tobacconists disappeared under a screaming mob of Russians. It reminded me of an exaggerated version of Pancake Day at Westminster School!

The Germans used their rifle butts on the seething mass of bodies, and the dog was let loose. In a few moments the mob had been cleared, and from the debris emerged Messrs Watson, Crump and Lewis – uninjured but very shaken.

The next item on the agenda was an identity parade, which meant standing in a queue once again before marching off to the station. Colonels and majors were separated from the rest of us, as they were to travel in third class carriages while we travelled in cattle trucks. This was no advantage as a third class carriage in Germany, with its hard and upright wooden seats, was even more uncomfortable than a cattle truck, where at least you could stretch your legs even if you couldn't see out of the window.

As we marched off to the station we were each issued with about half a foot of Würst sausage, and a number of unopened Red Cross parcels were put into the guard's van in case the journey should take longer than expected. The general opinion was that we would be in the trucks at least four days and nights if we were going to Czechoslovakia.

We boarded the train at four in the afternoon, having been kept hanging round on a series of futile parades for seven hours.

The cattle trucks were definitely above average, and the Germans had made some effort to make them more comfortable. There was a thick layer of straw on the floor, and a big stove in the middle of the truck was a welcome addition against the cold. If the number in each truck had been limited to twenty we would have had quite a comfortable journey, but unfortunately thirty-seven of us, plus two German guards, had to share the space for five days and four nights.

It seemed an interminable journey of stops and starts. At every junction we were shunted from one train to another, and the shunting engines seemed to take a delight in giving our trucks an extra savage jerk to make quite sure that everyone was awake. There was only one narrow window, which had been cut down the side of the truck, and reading or card-playing was virtually impossible. By carefully packing ourselves crossways on the floor, like sardines in a tin, there was just enough room for everyone to lie down, provided the two German sentries remained seated on their bench. My legs very nearly stretched the width of the cattle truck, so Dick Black and Arthur Gilbey, who were lying opposite me, had my feet level with their faces for most of the journey – a most unpleasant addition to the other discomforts.

We were fortunate in having two very good sentries, who were just as anxious as we were that the truck should be kept warm and got out at every station to beg, borrow or steal coal from any nearby engine. The unfortunate men had to sit up all night, and they combined the job of stoker with their other duties. They were both Austrian, and made no effort to conceal the fact that they were heartily sick of the war; when we reminded them that Hitler was also Austrian, they replied that they were ashamed of the fact. When we stopped at the bigger stations, they got out and bought us beer in exchange for cigarettes or soap. Our longest stop was at Dresden, where we were allowed out of the trucks to walk up and down the platform. It was difficult to see much of the town, but it appeared to be a depressing sort of place.

After we had been travelling for three days, our meagre ration of food had run out, so the German officer in charge of the train decided to issue the Red Cross parcels. This was contrary to the orders of the higher command, and the German officer was most anxious that we finish any food we drew from the parcels before we arrived at our destination.

The German forecast proved correct, and we arrived at our destination, Märisch Trubau, after travelling for five days and four nights. A large group of guards was awaiting our arrival at the station, and after being pushed about like cattle in the station yard we were marched through the dimly lit streets of Märisch Trubau with Tony Watson and Crump Colbeck giving an excellent rendering of 'Lulu, I Would Not Fool You'.

Considering the discomfort of the journey, morale was high.

9

Oflag VIIIF: Märisch Trubau

Märisch Trubau was a small town on the border of what were once Moravia and Bohemia, a hundred and twenty-five miles east of Prague. The town contained nothing worthy of mention, beyond a series of churches each more hideous than the last. The population was a mixture of Sudeten Germans and Czechs, with the former in the majority.

Oflag VIIIF was just outside the town, and as we marched from the station the usual speculation took place about the type of camp we should find on arrival. We had not long to wait before our new prison loomed out of the darkness; our first view of the brightly lit building was not unfavourable. The efforts to black out the windows had failed dismally, and from a short distance the building resembled a large hotel. There was a general sigh of relief that the Oflag was not a hutted camp.

When we had passed through the gate we noticed that the large main building was surrounded by a series of brick built bungalows, giving the camp area the appearance of a village.

Once again we queued up, and once again we were searched, but by this time we knew how to deal with the German soldiers, and a few cigarettes slipped across the table satisfied any curiosity regarding the contents of our baggage. We were then told to sort ourselves into groups of eight, sixteen or twenty-five with the people with whom we wished to share a room. I managed to get in a room for eight with Dick Black, Arthur Gilbey, Gussie Pearce, Donald Astley Cooper, Jack Comyn, John Berry and Desmond Haslehurst. We had all been at Fontanellato together, except for Desmond, who had been at another camp in Italy.

Our room on the first floor of the main building was twenty-two feet long and thirteen feet wide, and had a large window running across one end. The room contained four double decker beds, a radiator and two sets of cupboards on either side of a door that led into another room for eight officers. In the centre of the room were two wooden tables and eight wooden stools. Two good electric lights hung down over each table.

This was our new home. It had not the class of Fontanellato but it might have been a great deal worse. A wash, a shave and some hot food, and the journey was soon forgotten.

When we entered the building a crowd of officers was standing on the stairway to watch our arrival. Many were from Fontanellato and had stories of adventure and recapture similar to our own. The majority of officers in the camp were from Chieti, the camp in the south of Italy where an incredible 'no escape' order had resulted in their all being recaptured and shipped to Germany. These officers were rather unkindly referred to as 'Marshall's Mugs' – the SBO at Chieti had been a Colonel Marshall. There were also a large number of recaptured officers from the senior officers camp at Viano, including Gussie Tatham and Keith Hillas, both of whom had been at Capua with me. Simon Ramsay, who had also been at Capua and who had gone with them to Viano, had managed to get through the lines and reached England in safety.

After four nights in a cattle truck, a double decker bed with seven bed boards and a sacking mattress filled with wood shavings seemed a great luxury, and I think most of us slept well our first night at Märisch Trubau.

The next morning we walked out into the snow to take a look at our surroundings. The main building, which before the war had been used as a training centre for cadets of the Czechoslovak army, looked like a modern factory. It was of grey stone, with four floors and a basement. The surrounding bungalows, built of yellow stone, were not as unattractive as the main building, but on the whole I think that living in the 'biscuit factory' (as we called the main building) was preferable to living in the bungalows, as the latter were somewhat crowded and uncomfortable. A long, yellow, one-storied building, known as the theatre block, looked out on to a swimming bath, which at the time of our arrival was being used for ice skating. At the top end of the prison village several bungalows were set aside for the Indian officers, who also had their own cook-house and mess room. The Red Cross sent special parcels for the Indians, the chief contents being curry and rice, which enabled their cooks to turn out dishes to suit their gastronomic and religious tastes. The Indians, among whom were many Sikhs, were a splendid lot of men whose smart appearance and excellent manners were beyond reproach. Their black beards and brightly coloured turbans were a contrast to the drab appearance of the average English prisoner.

The exercise field between the biscuit factory and the public road contained a football ground and what had once been a tennis court; a path circled the field. The majority of the bungalows were arranged in two main streets running parallel to the football field on the other side of the building, the others being scattered around the theatre block and swimming bath. The cookhouse and two large dining rooms were at the back of the main building. The dining rooms were only used for lectures and special regimental dinners, as lack of equipment made central messing impossible. We had our meals in our rooms – hot drinks, boiled potatoes and other items from the German ration being prepared by the cookhouse and collected by the various rooms. As usual, the main part of our meal was derived from Red Cross parcels.

A gymnasium and hospital completed the amenities of our village, which covered about fifteen acres inside the wire and was inhabited by 1850 prisoners of war.

Our first two days in Oflag VIIIF were spent in drawing Red Cross clothing, getting registered by the British and German authorities in the camp, and having our photographs and finger-prints taken by the Germans. The photographs were rather amusing, as we had to sit on a stool holding a slate in front of us, on which was written our prisoner of war number. The Germans then stuck the photos on our prisoner identity cards, together with our fingerprints. Soon after having my photo taken, I took part in a play which necessitated my growing a moustache. The Germans noticed this at an identification parade and made me have my photograph taken again. As soon as the play finished, my moustache was removed and the Germans gave me up as a bad job.

The theatrical entertainments at Oflag VIIIF were of a very high standard. There were two theatres – the Gate Theatre in the outside theatre block and the Little Theatre on the second floor of the main building. The Gate had an excellent stage and orchestra pit that had been built by the French who had occupied the camp before our arrival. Our own technicians made many improvements, the most important being the manufacture of armchair seats for every member of the audience. These were made from wooden crates in which the Canadian Red Cross parcels arrived. The theatre could accommodate 120 in comfort – all that was now required was some good actors, and in this respect we were extremely fortunate.

The management and direction of the Gate Theatre was in the hands of officers from Chieti, who had discovered first class talent during their sojourn in Italy. Those of us who had arrived from other camps certainly benefited from their experience. The production, stage managing and lighting were carried out by people who really understood their job, and the scenery effects produced by the stage props department, from very limited material, exceeded the most optimistic expectations. The clothes, especially the 'girls' dresses, were of an even higher standard than those we had seen at Fontanellato, and made one wonder what these prison experts could do if they had unlimited material and machinery.

The first play I saw there was *Spring Meeting*, which had enjoyed considerable success in London. The production and acting in this Irish comedy were first class, an outstanding success being achieved by Captain James Macfarlane, who took the part of the leading lady. His appearance was received with a gasp of astonishment by those of us who had not seen him on stage before. It was hard to believe that we were not looking at a very chic lady! His blond hair, which he had allowed to grow long for the part, had been cleverly curled and arranged, and his figure (with a few additions), legs and feet were exactly those of a woman. His acting throughout was magnificent.

We came away from the show with the feeling that if this was the quality of Gate Theatre performances we were in for some good entertainment. We were not to be disappointed.

A musical comedy with full orchestra, entitled *Over the Sticks*, followed. This show was written and produced by Ian Tennant and included a full male and 'female' chorus. The acting, singing, dancing and general fooling were of a high order. I am sure that the London evening papers would have described the show as a 'lavish production'. The orchestra, under the direction of Maurice Butler, added considerably to the success of the show, which for two hours took us right away from the wire.

The Gate Theatre productions ran for ten days, enabling about twelve hundred people to see the performance.

Three other plays, *Blithe Spirit*, *I Have Been Here Before* and *The Corn is Green*, were produced at the Gate, and they all kept up the high standard already set.

After his success with *Over the Sticks*, Ian Tennant launched an even more lavish production entitled *Hollywood Cavalcade*, supported by an enlarged and improved addition of Tommy Sampson's band. *Hollywood Cavalcade* gave its audience a review of the silver screen during the last twenty years; the scenery included the inside of a palace, the deck of an American battleship and the dockside of New York harbour with the Queen Mary steaming majestically past the Statue of Liberty.

The German authorities, who were not helpful in other matters, gave the theatre a certain amount of assistance, procuring wigs for the female parts and endless paper for the scenic effects. English cigarettes proved a valuable currency in the town, and an active black market trade was carried on with the German soldiers and Czech workmen inside the camp.

I had always wanted to try my hand at amateur theatricals, and the talented performances at the Gate Theatre gave me the urge to get behind the footlights. I told the members of my room of my stagestruck condition and instructed them to make it known that I wanted a part, even if it was only the hind legs of a horse. They were not optimistic of my chances but did their best to get my ambitions known in the right quarters. Nothing transpired for several days and I was beginning to lose hope of even the horse's hind legs, when suddenly a dazzling offer dropped from the skies.

I was playing bridge one afternoon when Mark Ogilvie Grant, one of the theatre's most accomplished scenery designers, walked in and asked me if I would play the part of the villain in an Edwardian melodrama to be produced by Willie Willshaw at the Little Theatre. I jumped at the offer, trumped my partner's ace and was happy. To jump straight from the horse's hind legs to the villain far exceeded my wildest dreams! The Little Theatre was still being constructed, and Willie Willshaw's production, entitled *The White Rose*, written by Peter Willes, was to mark the opening.

Peter Willes, an officer in the 12th Lancers, had been badly wounded in the leg and foot, which necessitated the toe of his boot being supported by a wire attached to a strap below the knee. At the outbreak of war he had been in Hollywood, where he had played several minor roles. Fair, good looking and musical, he had a fine sense of humour and a flair for writing amusing sketches.

He had written *The White Rose*, a burlesque of *Bitter Sweet*, with the idea that the audience should treat it in the same spirit as London audiences had treated the production of *Young England* – that is to say, freely expressing their feelings during the play by such actions as booing the villain, cheering the hero and heroine and making any other demonstrations they considered suitable. This offered wide scope for wisecracks from the audience, and provided they entered into the spirit of the entertainment *The White Rose* had every chance of a successful ten-day run at the Little Theatre.

We had a month to learn and rehearse our parts. Willie and Peter were charming people to work with and were most patient over my lack of acting knowledge. I played the part of the wicked Earl of Buick; Peter Willes was the Duchess of Axminster. The funniest moment of the play was when Bill Bows, the Yorkshire fast bowler, appeared as a baby about to die from undernourishment. His last words before expiring in his cot were 'Muther, I 'ear 'arps' – which Bill put across in his best Yorkshire accent!

This melodrama, exhibiting with breathtaking rapidity the changes of Fortune's wheel, offered great scope to the actors and audience, and the latter were not slow to take their chance.

Tony Watson acted as prompter and sat on a stool in front of the footlights wearing an immense collar with a stock and a straw hat. His black hair was parted in the middle, and a scarlet nose and drooping moustache gave him a grotesque appearance. His handling of the obstreperous audience and his asides to the actors were delightfully funny. At times the play would be held up for several seconds while Tony implored the audience to keep quiet, and they in turn shouted at him to sit down. During these interruptions the unfortunate actors had to keep a straight face – at times very difficult.

The play was a resounding success. The final night coincided with my birthday, and after the show we had a supper party in my room, where Arthur Gilbey excelled himself as a chef.

We certainly had splendid entertainments at VIIIF, as in addition to the theatres we were provided with concerts by three different orchestras – a symphony orchestra conducted by Maurice Butler, an accordion orchestra led by Claude Godwin and a dance orchestra led by Tommy Sampson.

There were also large-scale educational facilities in the camp. Arthur Gilbey, Jack Comyn and I started to learn Russian. Arthur had already studied the language in Italy, and he undertook to coach me in the early stages. I fear I was a dull pupil, but Arthur was a hard taskmaster and used to dig me in the ribs with a stick when I made frequent errors with Russian grammar. I have since come to the conclusion that I shall never master Russian!

Most of our evenings were spent playing bridge or poker. The standard of bridge was fairly high, as many prisoners devoted a considerable period of their captivity to mastering the various conventions laid down by Culbertson and other bridge experts. Dick Black, a steady and long-suffering player, kindly agreed to take me on as a partner and we fixed up several engagements every week. It proved a happy combination, as neither of us took the game very seriously and Dick readily forgave my numerous aberrations.

In addition to bridge and poker there was a casino, run by ten officers in one of the outside bungalows. The casino was open twice a week, once for faro and once for card roulette. The casino evenings were great fun, and had quite a Monte Carlo atmosphere about them. Those of us who lived in the main building had to be back from the casino by 9.30 p.m. or we were liable to be mauled by the German dogs, which prowled round the camp after that hour.

When I was at Märisch Trubau I heard an amusing story about a camp police dog. The Italians, learning of the success of the German police dogs, decided to introduce them in one of their camps where the British officers were somewhat unruly. On one of the parades the officers failed to obey Italian orders, whereupon the commandant announced that he would let the dogs out. The arrival of the dogs was awaited with interest; after a few minutes a rather fat bloodhound waddled on to the parade ground. His arrival was greeted with ironic cheers and it was not long before he was being patted and stroked by the officers into whom he was meant to strike terror. The dog then ambled off into one of the huts and after a few minutes returned to the parade ground wearing sunglasses and a Balaclava helmet!

One of the padres at Märisch Trubau, who had been a prisoner since Dunkirk, recounted several amusing incidents that had occurred since he had been in captivity. At one camp the prisoners threw food over the wire to the German police dogs. The next day the Germans put up a notice which ran as follows: 'British officers must not throw food to the German dogs. The German dogs have been forbidden to eat any food thrown to them by British officers.'

The strangest story the padre told us concerned an RAF officer at Warburg camp, who for a wager pushed a ping pong ball round the three-quarter-mile perimeter of the camp with his nose! The feat took nine hours and the officer won his bet. His nose and knees had been specially strapped with plaster for the event.

At an other ranks camp near Berlin a certain number of prisoners were allowed to visit the city on so many days during the week. They soon started a black market in English cigarettes among the shops they visited, and were thus able to procure goods unattainable by the average Berlin citizen. Their appearance and general bearing were so good that after a time a letter was written to the German commandant complaining that the English soldiers resembled members of an army of occupation more than prisoners of war. Coming events cast their shadows before them!

The SBO at Oflag VIIIF was Colonel Waddilove. The position of SBO at a camp in Germany where there were nearly two thousand officers was not one to be envied, and we were lucky to have an officer who religiously defended our rights and who refused to cooperate with the Germans unless they cooperated with us. We saw very little of the German commandant, but we gathered that he was a typical Prussian who showed violent fits of temper unless he had his own way. The officers under his command were fairly harmless; one of them, an Austrian who counted our company at roll call, was quite a pleasant individual. The German soldiers were of a very low standard, ranging in age from sixteen to sixty-five. There was a sprinkling of the old regular type who had been wounded in Russia or Africa, but the remainder looked almost as ridiculous as the Italians. Their uniforms were old and patched and some of the older men looked as if they had been taken straight from agricultural jobs and put into uniform.

The most remarkable achievement at VIIIF was the manufacture and concealment of a wireless, on which we were able to get the BBC. Wireless experts in the camp collected enough material from the Czechs to construct a set that never failed to give us daily news bulletins. How the set was made or where it was hidden, I never discovered. In circumstances where secrecy is absolutely essential, ignorance is bliss. The method of hiding the set was practically search-proof and was the same as that adopted in other camps in Germany where wireless sets had been constructed. The BBC news was read out to each room in the evenings. During the reading, the passages and stairs were picketed with watchers who gave warning if any German appeared in the vicinity. The news office was a splendidly run concern, and the value of being able to get the proper news from home was inestimable. The wireless was always referred to as the 'Canary', and the reading of the Canary news was the high spot of the day.

The escape committee was run by Colonel David Stirling. Uniforms, documents, maps and other aids to escape were manufactured on a large scale. After much bad luck the efforts of the escape committee, always referred to as the 'cloak and dagger men', was rewarded by the successful escape of four officers.

The first attempt at escape ended in disaster. A number of officers were being moved to another camp, and it was arranged that one of them should jump from the train. The necessary maps, documents and money were supplied, and the officer managed to jump while others distracted the sentries' attention. But the train was travelling too fast, and the escaper broke his back, tragically dying on the way back to hospital.

The second attempt was also unsuccessful, but happily did not end in any loss of life. An officer was stowed away in a laundry basket and left the camp with the dirty linen. Unfortunately, the Germans altered their usual procedure, which resulted in the escaper mistiming his exit from the basket. Thinking that he had reached the point to leave the cart, he opened the lid of his basket and jumped out, only to find himself surrounded by German guards.

The third attempt at escape was most daring and managed to succeed at the third effort. The Russians who worked in the camp were usually marched in and out through one of the gates by a single German guard. It was decided to dress five officers as Russian prisoners and a sixth as a German guard. The 'guard' was to march the Russians out of a side gate in the wire while one of our rugby matches, always watched by a large crowd, was in progress. The gate, which was close to one of the sentry platforms, was always locked, but one of the escapers had studied the lock and was confident of opening it with a wire key. Few people outside the escape committee knew of the attempt and little attention was paid to the party as they wended their way past the crowd. They reached the gate under the very nose of the German sentry, but when the officer dressed as a German advanced to open the gate, the lock would not move. The sentry on the platform called out, but everyone kept their heads and the 'escort' answered him in German, marching his little party back to the main building without detection.

A further study was made of the lock, and three days later the attempt was made again. Once more the lock would not yield, and once more the party managed to return without arousing the suspicions of the Germans.

The third and last attempt proved successful. The lock yielded and the 'German' and his 'Russians' walked off to freedom. It was a splendid effort and one which called for the utmost patience and steady nerves. Two of the six were later recaptured, but the remaining four made good their escape and set off to get in touch with Czech agents in the neighbourhood of Prague. (The fate that overtook these officers will be related in the next chapter.)

The chief bone of contention between the German authorities and the inmates of VIIIF lay in the practice of snooping adopted by the Germans. The expression 'snooping' requires some explanation.

In prisoner of war camps, the detaining power occasionally carries out a search of the prisoners' rooms or other apartments in the camp in order to discover any efforts at escape, such as tunnelling, or to find weapons or tools that might be used for this purpose. This practice is acknowledged as being within the rules of the game, provided that the search party is accompanied by an officer. The Germans at Märisch Trubau sent out small search parties of their soldiers without an accompanying officer, and this infringement of the rules was known as snooping. The SBO protested to the German commandant about this, and as the latter paid no attention anti-snooping parties were organized in the camp. It was their duty to follow the German search parties wherever they went. The deadlock on this subject resulted in a fantastic state of affairs, as wherever the two or three inquisitive Germans walked in the camp, they were followed at a distance of two or three paces by a similar number of English officers. It was difficult to decide who looked the more ridiculous, the snoopers or the anti-snoopers. Whenever the Germans approached a bungalow or building, the officers tracking them ran ahead and warned the inmates by shouting 'Goon up!' The German soldiers were always referred to as 'Goons', but I have never been able to discover the origin of the expression.

The first result of the anti-snooping parties was that two officers taking part infuriated the German soldiers so much that they were ordered to appear before the commandant. A large demonstration was immediately arranged to coincide with the visit. A large black banner, similar to those carried in processions in Hyde Park, and bearing the words JOIN THE ANTI-SNOOPERS LEAGUE was carried by two officers, one wearing a grey bowler and the other a yellow straw hat. The standard bearers were followed solemnly by about two hundred officers, marching in threes. The arrival of the procession at the main gate of the camp coincided with the arrival of the commandant, who drove up in a bright yellow dog cart drawn by two horses. The sight of the fat commandant sitting bolt upright in his dog cart was too good to be true, and his equipage arrived at the gate to the sounds of *Gone Away*, blown on a hunting horn. The commandant was somewhat nonplussed by his reception, which was followed by a storm of ironical cheers. He completely lost his head when an officer stepped forward with a perfect replica of a full-size movie camera, turning the handle as he focused it on the commandant. The latter, thinking for a moment that the camera must be real, drew himself up in typical German fashion to pose for the picture. The demonstration had certainly proved very amusing, both to us and to the majority of the Germans present.

Our relations with the commandant did not improve, and a further incident occurred when the Germans tried to stage a snap identity roll call. The normal procedure was that we had two roll calls a day, one in the morning and one in the evening. The SBO considered that these two roll calls were quite sufficient, and as the German commandant would not cooperate over other matters, instructions were issued that no one was to pay attention to the German order to form up for the identity roll call, which entailed appearing with our identity discs and being compared to the photographs on our identity cards.

The German order to form up came through at about eleven o'clock, but none of us moved out of their rooms. The German officers walked up and down, and the guards fell in to their usual positions on the stairs and round the gymnasium, but no one appeared. The commandant completely lost his temper and raved at the SBO, who regretted that it was impossible for him to get the officers on parade. The Germans were kept waiting three hours before the SBO gave the order to get on parade. The Germans never tried the experiment again.

April sunshine began to bring out the backward buds of spring. The girls from the nearby Nazi women's camp danced around the town football field in dark blue pants and white blouses (always watched by a large crowd of officers) and the Russians were still advancing. A spirit of optimism prevailed, and spring was in the air.

Bungalow gardens were planted with lettuces and spring onions; the sun shone, and the more hardy members of the camp bathed in the swimming pool.

An alcoholic drink made from raisins, sugar, beer and yeast made its appearance in certain rooms, which at night resounded with cries of revelry. An occasional stool or table hurtled through the windows, no doubt aimed at the patrolling dog.

Yes – things were looking up. Dick and I decided that our room should be springcleaned, and with the help of Gussie Pearce and Donald Astley Cooper, we scrubbed the ceiling, walls and floor. It was hard work, and we were proudly surveying our handiwork when the company adjutant, Mike Savill, walked into the room and told us that the camp was being moved to Germany in two days' time. Our observations on this interesting piece of news are unprintable.

The forthcoming move gave ample scope for rumour, and we were not slow off the mark. Various theories were put forward about the reasons for the move, the more optimistic being the threat of Russian liberation. The prophets found no difficulty in naming our destination – from the very first, rumour singled out the Brunswick area as our new address, and in this respect it was, unusually, accurate.

The journey was not viewed with much relish, as reports of the nightly RAF attacks on the German railway system indicated that a night spent in a siding would not be without its dangers. The Brunswick area itself also seemed to be a happy hunting ground for our planes.

The Germans had decided to move the camp lock, stock and barrel; even the electric light bulbs were taken with us. On 26 April large lorries drove into the camp, and the advance guard of the furniture was loaded on to them.

A colonel and another two hundred soldiers arrived in Märisch Trubau. The colonel was to be our commandant at the new camp and he had the reputation of getting what he wanted. We were told that it would take at least a week to move the inmates of the camp, together with the mass of tables, stools, cupboards and other odd bits of furniture, which indicated a shortage of this type of article in Germany.

David Stirling and Jack Pringle (another member of the cloak and dagger setup) were determined to hide up in the camp, and when everyone had left to escape from the area and join certain contacts in

Czechoslovakia. This meant that two other officers had to take their places when it came to their turn to depart. A similar plan was arranged for one or two other members of the organization, and it was hoped that if enough officers changed identity cards, it would so fluster the already harassed camp authorities that they would give it up as a bad job and merely concentrate on numbers rather than individuals.

The first party left the camp on 28 April, after the normal search and identity parade. Several identities had been changed, and as expected the Germans had not the time to worry about it, allowing the 'stand-ins' to pass through.

Arthur Gilbey and Jack Comyn stood in for David Stirling and Jack Pringle, and although the Germans were aware that they were not the true owners of these identity cards they let them through. In the meantime, David and Jack Pringle took Arthur and Jack Comyn's place in our room. It was their plan to stay on until the final day and then hide in one of the bungalow attics. They arranged to remain until the last, but they were discovered by the Germans in one of their searches. However, two other members of the 'C and D' managed to remain concealed and made good their escape after we had left. Frank Wallace, another enthusiastic member, hid in a trench in the football field, but was run to earth on the last night by one of the prowling Alsatians, with whom he very wisely did not attempt to dispute matters!

Our company left on the morning of 1 May. After a hurried breakfast we carried our baggage to the gymnasium, where the search and identity check took place. The search caused little trouble; a few English cigarettes to the German soldiers and no questions were asked. We were kept hanging about for two hours and then set off, with a strong guard, to march to the station, weighed down by our parcels, blankets, overcoats and other impediment.

Donald Astley Cooper and Gussie Pearce provided an amusing spectacle, as in addition to their ordinary baggage they carried four panels of wood with which to make an armchair on arrival; Donald also had a saxophone and clarinet. Halfway to the station, this bundle of assorted articles came apart and the contents fell all over the road, much to the amusement of their less heavily burdened companions. However, they managed to reach the station without loss, and the armchair later proved well worth the trouble.

Major Anton Hathorn and his South African officers had so

many odds and ends to transport that they constructed a wooden coffin with a handle at each end, into which they piled crockery, bread, jam, shoes and a variety of other equipment. The weight proved too much for them and they frequently had to stop and change hands. In order to get over this difficulty while marching through the town, the perspiring Hathorn turned himself about and marched down the street backwards, much to the astonishment of the inhabitants.

On arrival at the station yard we were divided up into groups of eighteen and taken off to the trucks. There we were addressed by one of the interpreters, who solemnly read out a notice from a typewritten sheet.

'As the British Government still reserves for itself the right of chaining German prisoners, the German Government claims a similar privilege. On recent train journeys many British officers have attempted to escape, in some cases attacking and even murdering their German guards. For this reason the German Army commander has ordered that all officers shall be handcuffed while journeying between camps . . .'

We greeted this ridiculous statement with shouts and laughter, and I did not listen to the rest of the oration. The thought of a five-day journey in handcuffs was not very pleasant, but no one could help laughing at the pompous stupidity of the Germans. Our smiles soon turned to oaths as we climbed into the cattle trucks and saw what awaited us.

On entering the truck we had to remove our boots and put them in a sack, and then one of the soldiers fixed on our handcuffs. One end of the truck, comprising only a third of the total floor space, had been wired off to make a cage nine feet long by eight feet wide, and eighteen of us were crammed into this totally inadequate space together with our baggage, which included Donald's musical instruments and Anton Hathorn's infernal coffin. There were five wooden benches in the cage, three round the walls and two up the centre, and by the time we were all in, it was quite impossible to move. Parcels were piled on the benches and floor, and as we were handcuffed it was very difficult to get ourselves in any sort of order. We were all pushing and shoving, tripping over parcels and generally getting tied up with the chains of our bracelets.

Anton, having told the German guard exactly what he thought of them and their country, then took command of the situation and gradually some sort of order was restored. Most of the parcels were hung from the ceiling, and the remainder were pushed under the benches; before the train started we were all able to sit down in some sort of position. The prospect of a long journey under these conditions was positively appalling, especially as the German order was that no one should be allowed out of the cage for any purpose whatsoever.

The other two thirds of the carriage were occupied by seven German guards, who were supplied with a special table for their comfort. One could not help being amused at the fact that eighteen bootless and handcuffed British officers in a wire cage required seven armed guards to look after them. The Germans may think us decadent but they also consider us dangerous!

It is to the everlasting credit of the British Army that, despite these extraordinary precautions, one officer managed to escape on the journey. I never discovered how it was done, but I understand that unlike our truck his compartment had a window through which he disappeared during the night.

It is to the everlasting discredit of the German Army that a party of British officers in our train who had passed the repatriation board, and several of whom were limbless, were made to travel in conditions similar to our own. When Major Knight, the senior officer among the disabled party, protested to the German commandant on the station, the latter flew into a rage and threatened to shoot unless Major Knight got into the truck before he counted three. There was nothing to do but comply, as an infuriated Prussian waving a revolver is no person to argue with, unless one is particularly tired of life.

The train did not leave the station until after lunch, by which time we were already suffering from acute discomfort. The prospect of the night did not even bear thinking about. The handcuff difficulty was soon solved, as Gussie Pearce discovered a method of unlocking them, which meant that we only wore them during the day, when the Germans were looking. The occupants of another truck hurled their handcuffs out of the window when the train was going at full speed. Another party put their bracelets in the tin drum which served as latrine and urinal, and when the Germans emptied it there was a shower of handcuffs on the line.

We started to plan positions for the night long before darkness fell, as it was touch and go whether there would be enough room on the floor for all of us to lie down. Eventually we pushed the two centre benches to the side of the truck, making a platform with the bench already running alongside the wall. Eight managed to sardine themselves at full length on the platform; seven others lay down with their heads by the opposite wall; Dick Black lay parallel with the wire; and Donald Astley Cooper and I somehow managed to squeeze underneath the platform of benches, where we spent a night of acute discomfort and semi-suffocation. The same sleeping arrangements were adopted the following night.

The journey, though abominably uncomfortable, did not prove as long or as dangerous as was expected. We reached a small station just outside Brunswick on the morning of 3 May, having been in the trucks for two days and two nights. When we were released from our cage we stepped over to collect our boots and politely handed our handcuffs back to the Germans, who were waiting to unlock them. I think we were entitled to consider that the last laugh was with us.

We left the station, and after marching for half a mile through a pine wood we entered the gates of a modern Luftwaffe barracks, part of which had been handed over for our occupation. The first thing we noticed were two buildings that had obviously been hit by bombs.

Life showed every prospect of becoming more exciting.

10

Oflag 79:
Brunswick

The first few days in our new camp at Brunswick – Oflag 79 –
were chaotic. No furniture had been left by the Luftwaffe and our
beds, tables, chairs and other belongings came through in dribs and
drabs from Märisch Trubau. When the first lorryloads of our
furniture arrived from the station, there was a mad scramble to seize
anything one could lay one's hands on, but after a day or two the
distribution of these precious articles was properly organized.

The camp consisted of four two-storied buildings of about eighty
yards in length standing on a wired-in enclosure of five acres. When
one considers the ground space taken up by the buildings and the
fact that there were some two thousand prisoners in the camp, it
becomes clear that there was not much space in which to move
about.

Brunswick was three miles south-west of the camp, and the
Brunswick aerodrome was separated from us by a narrow belt of
pine trees. The surrounding countryside was flat and uninteresting,
and we could see a considerable distance from the attic windows of
one of our buildings.

The erection of the wire had not been completed when we
arrived. A large number of the German Labour Corps were
employed to finish the job as soon as possible. The majority of these
workmen were foreigners and included French, Poles, Czechs and
Danes. We had ample opportunity to talk with the workmen, whose
opinion of Hitler appeared to be very similar to our own. The
continual coming and going of these workmen, who wore white
overalls and the German military cap, was responsible for the first
attempt at escape.

Archie Orr-Ewing, Archie Noel, Tom Bond, 'Brockie' Mytton
and MacWilliams had arrived with the first party from Märisch
Trubau and had taken careful note of the method by which the
parties of workmen came in and out of the camp. They decided to
dress up as workmen and attempt to escape. Archie Orr Ewing,

who spoke fluent German, had managed to procure a German overcoat; he was to dress up as a German NCO and the others were to make overalls from their sheets. The party was to be marched out of the main gate by Archie Orr Ewing at a time when the workmen were going in and out of the camp. If they succeeded in getting out, they would try to jump a train and get to France.

The whole exploit was undertaken in a spirit of levity, with the hope that Fortune would be on their side. Unfortunately, most of the workmen were very small, whereas Orr Ewing, Bond and MacWilliams were of medium size, while Brockie and Archie Noel were tall. The clothes were soon made by the 'C and D' clothing experts, and the day after their completion was selected for the attempt. Archie Orr Ewing's disguise was perfect, and the overalls supplied for the others were very similar to those worn by the workmen. Brockie was wearing grey overalls that Dick Black had brought from Italy. His broad figure, reinforced by the provisions he was concealing, gave him a somewhat unusual appearance.

The party moved off to the gate soon after luncheon. Archie said something to the sentry in charge, the gate was opened and the strange party of workmen walked out to freedom. They turned right outside the gate, following the road that led through the pine trees to the station. After walking a few paces they passed a German officer; Archie saluted him and he returned the compliment. A few more yards and they would have been round the corner among the pine trees. Then the worst happened. A German soldier, who had seen a lot of the party at Märisch Trubau, noticed who they were and brought them back inside the wire. It had been a good, though short-lived attempt. The party was taken off to the cooler, where they remained for ten days.

Another, somewhat unorthodox, attempt at escape was made within two days of our arrival. Malise Cruickshanks clung to the underneath of a lorry as it drove out of the camp. He was immediately spotted by a sentry, who fired his rifle into the ground close to the vehicle. Malise was then unhitched and also removed to the cooler.

Our new accommodation was hopelessly inadequate. Rooms constructed to hold ten people had as many as twenty-five officers sleeping, eating and living in them. The camp itself was well built, and had every modern convenience, but these advantages were cancelled by the overcrowding.

It was not unnatural that since the indignities of our journey from Märisch Trubau our relations with the German commandant were on the worst possible footing. As soon as we arrived, the SBO had an interview with the commandant. He lodged complaints about the journey, the present accommodation and the fact that the camp was situated next to a military objective. He also demanded an interview as soon as possible with the Protecting Power. The last demand was granted but the other complaints were sidestepped. The SBO gave the Germans a shock when he announced that the two American officers in the camp were sending a protest through the Protecting Power to their own Government regarding their treatment on the train. It was apparent from the commandant's embarrassment that he had been unaware there were Americans in our party. The German proclamation regarding handcuffing did not apply to Americans. The SBO always held his ground in his interviews with the commandant, and although they usually ended in a deadlock they at least showed our Prussian keeper that bullying methods were no good.

Despite the uncomfortable conditions we soon settled down to the usual routine existence. The churches, the theatre, the casino and other amenities were soon in action. In the evenings the camp echoed with the music of Tommy Sampson's band, and brightly coloured notices announced forthcoming attractions at the theatre.

Everyone was anxious to find out if the RAF and American Air Force were aware that we were in the Brunswick area. Large-scale daylight raids were taking place each day. A Luftwaffe barracks next door to Brunswick aerodrome offered an obvious target, by day or by night. The German authorities assured us that Geneva had been informed, and this statement was proved to be true when certain letters were forwarded to the correct address. I must admit that I had complete faith in the RAF and the American Air Force. Modern bombing methods, if we were to believe all we had been told, should lead to no mistakes. When the bombers came over I was always convinced that nothing would fall on the camp. How wrong I was!

We saw hundreds of American heavy bombers pass over, and the nearby anti-aircraft batteries fired everything they had at them. It was most cheering for us to see the complete mastery of the sky that the Allies had now attained. When the barrage became heavy we had to take cover from the falling shrapnel, and many officers descended to the cellars. Dick Black, whose faith in the accuracy of our bombing was not as great as mine, used to get inside our tin clothes cupboard; if a bomb had fallen on our building, I have no doubt that he would have been retrieved unscathed from his somewhat unusual shelter.

The first night raid on Brunswick came uncomfortably near the camp. The sirens sounded soon after midnight, and within a few minutes the camp was lit up by a series of yellow flares dropped from the planes. This was the crucial test. Were the planes dropping flares to light up the target or were the flares a 'keep off' sign to the aircraft following?

It was, to say the least, an interesting moment. There was a large exodus to the cellars, but Dick and I stayed in our double decker bed smoking cigarettes and hoping for the best. It was a cold night, and I persuaded Dick that his cupboard would be both cold and uncomfortable. The anti-aircraft barrage was terrific and we could hear the bombs crashing on Brunswick. No bombs fell near the camp. I think that night raid proved to many that the RAF knew where we were.

The first daylight raids were uneventful, with the exception of one that caused an amusing incident. Two American fighters, returning from escorting bombers to attack Berlin, swooped low over the camp and machine-gunned the airfield. Several officers who were sunbathing in a state of semi-nudity made a rush for cover and jumped through a basement window, rudely interrupting a discussion by the theological society on Christian worship.

After we had been at Brunswick for three weeks two more officers, Charles Duvivier and Dick Napier Martin, made a daring attempt at escape. Choosing a very dark night of wind and rain, they cut a hole in the wire within a few yards of the sentry standing outside the German guard room. Unnoticed, they crawled through the wire and got away. Charles Duvivier was to make for Belgium, where he had relations, and Dick Napier Martin was, I think, going to make his way to France.

Unfortunately they were both recaptured the next day and shut up in Brunswick civil gaol for ten days, where they did solitary confinement on very meagre rations. The Germans did not announce their recapture until the day before they returned to the camp. We had begun to think that they had made good their escape. They returned in good health but definitely thinner.

Their treatment had been good compared with that received by other officers who had been retaken by the Germans. One officer in the camp had been captured when on a special mission in Yugoslavia. He was taken to the prison in Belgrade, condemned to death and locked in a dark cell for ten days. His clothes were taken from him and he was given a blanket to sleep in. He was exercised in a corridor where the previous week the Germans had shot two other British prisoners. After ten days of hell, his death sentence was cancelled and he was sent to our camp.

These first-hand stories of Belgrade prison were bad, but even worse ones were to follow when two of the officers who had escaped from Märisch Trubau dressed as Russians returned to our camp after spending several days in the Gestapo gaol in Prague. They had managed to reach Prague, but the population was so completely cowed by the terror of the Gestapo that no one dared help them. They were recaptured and handed over to the Gestapo.

Our officers reported that the gaol was full of political prisoners, male and female. The corridors rang day and night with the cries of people being tortured. The women were looked after by special female Gestapo who carried truncheons and revolvers. They stripped the unfortunate women prisoners and beat them across the breasts and thighs with whips; as one officer observed, their behaviour was even more bestial than that of their male companions, if that was possible.

If a prisoner would not give the information the Gestapo required – and in many cases they had no information to give – they were hung naked from their wrists with the tips of their toes just touching the ground. If this failed, they were beaten insensible and thrown back into their cells. Their diet was so arranged that after a year's imprisonment the prisoner died. To make absolutely sure of this, they were made to do twenty-five minutes of violent exercise a day.

With the arrival of the two officers from Prague, two of the six who had escaped from Märisch Trubau remained to be accounted for. One had been recaptured within a week of the escape; another was known to be hiding up with a farmer in Moravia. It was hoped that the remaining two had got into contact with the Czech underground movement. But alas, our hopes and good wishes for these adventurers were soon shattered. The German commandant sent for the SBO and informed him that the two remaining officers had been shot while attempting to escape after recapture. He added that their ashes would arrive for burial in due course. The SBO asked the Protecting Power to make the fullest inquiries regarding the death of these two officers, but mention of their ashes indicated the work of the Gestapo. Nothing was ever discovered regarding their deaths.

If they were in prison in Prague they could not possibly have attempted to escape and any attempt on the journey in a prison train was equally impossible. There is little doubt that the Gestapo had shot them. It was a tragic end to a brave adventure.

We managed to procure a certain amount of information regarding the Derby runners from our weekly newspaper, *The Camp*, and from letters received from home. We pasted up a list of runners and prices, and accepted bets in sterling or camp marks.

Betting on a far more important event – the Invasion – had been going on for weeks. The gamblers had reaped a rich harvest in May, the month that most people had thought would produce the long-awaited event. During the first week of June the Invasion was the sole topic of conversation. Finally, a German sentry announced that the great event had started at long last. As the same gentleman had informed us correctly about the fall of Rome, verification from the 'Canary' was eagerly awaited. On the afternoon of 6 June a special bulletin was sent round after lunch giving us the BBC announcement of the landing in Normandy.

It was a great moment, and the fact that the enormous casualties expected had not materialized made the news even more splendid. A great moment: the first milestone towards our deliverance.

11

Raids and restlessness

The final phase of prisoner of war life started with the Allied invasion of the Continent. The starter's gun had been fired; the race had begun. For the thousands of prisoners behind the wire, the only question was, 'How many days, weeks or months before the end?' It was only natural that the majority of prisoners of war were over-optimistic and apt to forget the weeks of preparation necessary before a large-scale advance could take place.

The last weeks of term are always the longest for the schoolboy, and so it is with the prisoner of war; the last few weeks of the Second World War seemed unutterably long. Mid-July 1944 saw us waiting for the end. The fantastic speed of the Russian advance had taken our breath away and seemed too good to be true. Meanwhile, the Allied forces on the Cherbourg peninsula were building up their strength for the push to Paris.

Life in the camp was without incident. The most ardent escape merchants were prepared to return home in a normal manner, and the tunnellers laid down their tools for good. We were marking time.

The weather, which had been cold and wet during June, took a turn for the better by the middle of July. The atmosphere in the crowded rooms became unbearably close at night. Dick Black and I decided to search for cooler sleeping quarters. By curtaining off the end of the passage in the attic of our building, we managed to arrange a cool and comfortable room.

On the morning of 21 July we were sitting in our new quarters when Arthur Gilbey came through the curtain and announced that he had some red-hot news that, for the moment, we must treat as confidential. We settled him on a stool and told him to let us have it – we could tell by his face that it was going to be something big.

An attempt had been made on Hitler's life; several of his generals had been killed – there was even a possibility that Hitler himself might be dead. But the cream of the BBC newsflash was the announcement that civil war had broken out in Germany.

Arthur had certainly brought us something big – we almost felt that the war was over. The official report was circulated round the camp during the lunch hour and the majority of us considered packing our bags.

Civil war! Just what we had long been hoping for. It could only be a matter of a week or more before the end. Our spirits rose to the skies, only to be completely dashed to the ground in the next forty-eight hours. Hitler was alive and kicking – the generals' plot had misfired. It will always remain a mystery to me why the BBC decided to announce that civil war had broken out. Civil war is a pretty powerful statement. Was it a shot in the dark backed up by some forceful wishful thinking? If so, it was very short of the mark. Perhaps it was part of a new method of propaganda intended only for foreign consumption. Looking at it purely from the point of view of prisoners of war in Germany, it had the worst possible effect on what were already overstrung nerves.

It took us several days to settle down after that eruption. The fighting in France seemed fairly static. The red ink that denoted any advance of our troops on the innumerable maps in the camp was gathering strength before flooding the paper towards Paris and the Seine. The Russians were in the suburbs of Warsaw, but were finding it a harder nut to crack than the other cities they had lately swallowed up. It was a period of tension during which Dick and I fully appreciated the seclusion of our attic.

The Germans had promised us when we first arrived that the camp would be enlarged as soon as they had repaired the bombed-out buildings that adjoined the prison compound. Four more houses and a further five acres of ground were added to the camp. On 4 August the order to expand was given. We were ordered to leave our attic, so we arranged to live with Johnny de Moraville, Paul and the two Archies.

The Germans arranged an intensive search during the move to the new quarters. Civil police and Gestapo arrived in the camp. Those moving were searched as they moved out of the old compound, and the following day everyone in the old area was made to spend the day in the new enclosure while the old houses were searched from top to bottom. On our way to the new enclosure we passed through the German officers' quarters, where the civil police and Gestapo were waiting to search us. The police were for the most part remarkably polite: in a few cases they attempted to put over some very clumsy propaganda about Jews and Bolshevism, which was treated with the contempt it deserved. They then moved over to the old buildings where they spent the rest of the day systematically searching each room, presumably in an attempt to locate the Canary.

It was while we were waiting among the pine trees before returning to our own quarters that we had our first serious air raid. It was a day of blue sky and bright sunshine – ideal conditions for a daylight raid. Soon after lunch the warning was sounded and hundreds of American heavy bombers appeared from every direction. It seemed that the planes were flying overhead on their way to another target – until the leaders of one formation dropped white smoke flares over the camp. Then the trouble started. We heard the scream of the first bombs falling. There was a general rush for cover and those unable to reach a building threw themselves flat on the ground. The falling bombs made a noise like an express train rushing through a station, and the earth shuddered and shook when they hit the ground. Johnny and I lay on our faces alongside the wall of one of the formerly demolished buildings. Wave after wave of planes roared overhead and the falling bombs crashed nearer and nearer the camp. When the last plane had passed over the camp was surrounded by dense clouds of smoke, but no bomb had fallen inside the wire. If this was precision bombing, it was definitely too precise for most of us. The targets had been the aerodrome on one side of the camp and the aircraft factory on the other; judging by the smoke, they had received pretty severe treatment. It was a nerve-racking ordeal that we all hoped would not be repeated. It was a most unpleasant sensation to be bombed when one was surrounded by wire and unable to get away. A stiff whisky and soda would have helped to calm the nerves, but the best we could get was a strong cup of tea.

A week later there was a heavy night raid on Brunswick, when according to the English communiqués twelve hundred tons of bombs were dropped on the town. No bombs fell very near the camp, but we could hear the sickening screech as they hurtled downwards on their voyage of death and destruction. The sky was lit up by the innumerable fires that started in the town, and wave after wave of our planes kept up the attack for over half an hour.

I watched the raid from my window, and as the tempo of destruction quickened I forgot that the Germans were our enemies; I forgot everything except the fact that this was the so-called civilization of 1944. I thought of women and children cowering in the cellars; the sick in hospital; the old and infirm. One deafening roar, and they would be no more. The war had to be won and the Germans deserved all they received, but I defy any man to be an observer of one of those big night raids on a city without feeling nauseated by civilian destruction.

On 21 August a batch of new prisoners arrived from the Western front, bringing us up-to-date details of the Invasion. They belonged to another army, which talked only in thousands – thousands of guns, thousands of tanks, thousands of ships, and thousands of planes. The sleeves of their battledress were covered in every conceivable sign, number and flash. One almost expected to find their home address on their cuffs. Their description of operations sounded like some story by H. G. Wells, and one very hard for most of us to picture. They certainly brought great news, which was backed up by the steady onward flow of bright red ink on the maps.

Shortly after the arrival of these new prisoners Colonel Wadilove, the SBO, David Stirling and Jack Pringle were removed to other camps. The commandant thus ended his battle with the SBO – an indication that the best man had won the day. David and Jack were known by the Germans to be connected with the 'C and D', and their record of attempted escapes from other camps presumably made them 'undesirable customers'. We were all sorry to see Colonel Wadilove go, as he had been a great champion of our rights. The unenviable position of SBO was taken on by Captain Micklethwaite, RN. His tenure of office was very short, as a few weeks later he too was sent to another camp. Colonel Brown, a young man who had been captured at Léros, stepped into his shoes.

The warm weather that had made its appearance at the end of July developed into a heatwave during August. The pine trees surrounding the camp seemed to suck away any available air, leaving us to scorch and gasp in the blazing sun. It was too hot to play cards in the evening, and the inside of the theatre was like a Turkish bath. From 17 to 24 August I was taking part in an Ian Tennant revue, *London Pride*. It is difficult to say who suffered most – the audience or the actors. The auditorium was like a furnace and a few minutes under the stage lights brought the performers to melting point. The production was not up to the standard of *Hollywood Cavalcade*, though the scenic effects reached new heights. The final curtain showed a background of Piccadilly Circus – complete with Eros, Guinness Time, and innumerable coloured electric signs switching on and off. The last night had to

166

be abandoned as a result of a shattering and fatal daylight raid during which part of the theatre was badly damaged.

I think most of us will remember 24 August for the rest of our days. The alarm sounded about 10.30 in the morning, and formations of American bombers soon approached the camp area. Once again, the leading planes dropped their target indicator flares almost over the camp and most people, remembering the earlier raid, went either to the cellars or to their rooms. A number of officers still had sufficient faith in precision bombing to remain outside and watch the proceedings from among the pine trees. I still felt that no bombs would drop inside the camp and I stood by the window in my room to watch the ack-ack bursting round the planes as they passed overhead. The noise was terrific. Buildings shook from top to bottom; the 'express trains' came hurtling from the sky, one after another, and seemed to be falling dangerously near. Suddenly, there was a terrific crash and I saw the lower half of the camp completely enveloped in black smoke and dust. That was enough for me – there was no more argument about precision bombing. I darted down to the cellar and joined the more sensible people who had been down there from the start.

I found Donald Astley Cooper, and we sat together on a disused stone lavatory seat, smoking cigarette after cigarette and occasionally blocking our ears with our hands as the explosions and blasts became more violent. On one or two occasions the cellar walls swayed so much we thought the whole building was going to collapse. At last the noise ceased, and we crawled like rats out of a hole to survey the damage.

It was an amazing sight. The camp was surrounded by fires and the roofs of two of our own buildings were alight. The German officers' quarters were blazing, as was the 'cooler', just outside the compound. Six bombs – estimated at between 500 lb and 1000 lb – had fallen inside the wire, together with a large quantity of incendiary and anti-personnel bombs. All this on ten acres in which there were eight large living houses and nearly two thousand people.

When we first came out of the cellars we imagined that many people must have been killed. As luck would have it most of the big bombs had fallen in the open, on the sandy soil among the pine trees, several of which had been uprooted and lay spreadeagled across the ground. The cookhouse – just inside the wire – had

received a direct hit and was completely demolished. Nearly all the
windows in the camp were smashed and the roofs had gaping holes
where incendiary and anti-personnel bombs had fallen. The smaller
trees dotted about the camp were snapped in two, and all the
buildings were scarred from top to bottom by fragments from the
anti-personnel bombs. A dead horse, with most of its innards blown
away, lay on the concrete just outside the wire. The German soldier
leading it had been killed. The camp was enveloped in a cloud of
smoke and dust. The earth was strewn with broken glass and tiles.

The most extraordinary escape was in the batmen's quarters,
where a heavy bomb had dropped right alongside the wall,
completely shattering the upper part of the building. The men, who
were all in the cellar, escaped injury.

When a check had been made it was discovered that three officers
had been killed, eight seriously injured and thirty slightly hurt. One
German officer and several German soldiers also lost their lives. It
was a miracle that more people were not killed considering the
number of bombs that had fallen on so small an area.

The main targets of the raid, the aerodrome and the aircraft
factory, were severely damaged. The camp had been the recipient of
bombs that had fallen short or beyond either target. Bombs do
strange things. A surrealist exhibition had been held in one of the
attics some time before the raid. Several of the posters had been left
on the beams. The only one untouched after the raid announced in
large red letters – LIFE IS A SERIES OF EXPLOSIONS. Too
true!

For several days after the raid the camp was in a state of chaos.
The drains were smashed, the electric light cables were broken and
the water was cut off. On the evening of the raid the only water
available was that obtained from leaks in the firemen's hoses as they
played them on the smouldering buildings. It was an amusing sight
to see groups of men squatting on the ground filling tins from the
little jets of water squirting from holes in the hoses. In some cases
the holes were enlarged – much to the fury of the firemen.

That evening the entertainment committee arranged an open-air
concert on the concrete walk outside our building. Tony Watson,
Mike Savill and Mark Ogilvie Grant, dressed as charwomen, gave
an excellent rendering of 'We Always Meet Our Troubles With A
Smile' and Tony Watson sang 'Any Old Iron' even quicker than
Harry Champion in his prime. The whole entertainment did much
to cheer us up and calm our nerves.

For the next week or so we had to make the best of a bad job. The pine trees that had been brought down by the bombs were cut up into firewood and a series of outside kitchens were started. Iron grills, bricks and other debris from the raid were all used, and within a day there were again excellent cooking arrangements. Only a limited amount of water was available. The Germans lent picks and shovels with which parties of energetic officers dug down to mend the drains. Unbroken tiles were collected and any mendable holes in the roofs were repaired. I think the Germans were quite impressed by the way we coped with a difficult situation.

The raid left its mark on the nerves of the camp. When the sirens sounded again – as they did day and night for the next few months – no one talked about precision bombing. Everyone went under cover, and the majority took to the cellars when the ack-ack started. The raids were very tiresome – especially at night – but we just had to put up with them.

In the first week of September twenty-seven officers who had been down for repatriation for over a year were warned that they would be going home some time within the next ten days. They had heard this story so often that they did not pay much attention to it. However, this time it proved correct, and on the evening of 6 September they left for the station to join the train that was to take them to Sweden. A large crowd saw them off at the gate, giving them innumerable messages for friends at home, the most important being one to the Air Ministry giving them the exact location of the camp! Peter Willis was among the party. He was a loss to the theatrical side of the camp, as he was by far the most accomplished actor.

It gave me a queer sensation to watch this party leave. They were walking away to home and freedom, while we stayed the other side of the wire like a lot of caged animals. In a way it hurt, but on the other hand everyone was delighted that these people who had suffered so much should be going home at last.

On 14 October Brunswick suffered another devastating raid. The planes arrived shortly before three in the morning and for twenty minutes all hell was let loose on the city. The camp was lit up by dozens of flares, and the buildings shook as each bomb exploded, though none fell within a mile of the camp.

Gas works, chemical works, a mine factory and a laundry all went sky high, together with about two square miles of buildings in and around the city. Thirty-three thousand people were rendered homeless, and several hundred were killed, including a large number who died of suffocation when the ventilator shafts of deep shelters were blown in. The fires burned for twenty-four hours, while firemen and young boys hacked their way among the ruins.

These tragedies were taking place day and night in Germany, and still they fought on. The civilians in Brunswick shrugged their shoulders and remarked, 'If you go to war you must expect this sort of thing.'

For the sake of one madman and a crooked cross – daily death and destruction on a scale that, ten years ago, no one in their worst nightmare could have envisaged.

October dragged on. Rain and cold soon displaced the mildness of early autumn. The sirens wailed day and night and the lights were turned off with maddening regularity. I slept in an alcove with Dick, Paul, the two Archies and Mark Ogilvie Grant. It had been delightfully cool during the hot days of summer, but it turned out to be an icehouse in winter. Dick and Brockie Mytton (who lived in another room) decided to build a stove in the alcove on which we could cook our meals and which we hoped would give some sort of heat to the room. Bricks, clay and a long piece of piping were procured from the bombed-out area, and Dick and Brockie then set to work. Their efforts were untiring but the great difficulty was to produce a stove that did not fill the place with smoke. After three attempts their efforts met with partial success. They built a large brick stove with room for frying and boiling, with a fair-sized oven at the back. Provided that the wind was blowing in the right direction, the stove did not smoke too badly and we managed to cook for sixteen people. Brockie cooked for his mess and I took over our cook's job from Archie Noel.

I had learnt quite a bit about cooking since my Capua days, but I still had not mastered my worst opponent – the tin opener. The weapon I was forced to use was even blunter than the Italian model, and in a few days my fingers showed the scars of battle.

The landing at Arnhem raised many hopes for a finish by Christmas. The sad but glorious failure of that effort damped the optimism of many; others remained confident of their Christmas dinner in England.

November came. The mud increased and the number of Red Cross parcels in the store began to dwindle. The issue was reduced to half a parcel a week per man, and for the first time for many months we began to get hungry. Empty stomachs had an astonishing effect on the behaviour of certain members of the camp; when they discovered that half a parcel did not supply enough food to satisfy their appetites they decided to steal food from their fellow prisoners. This regrettable lapse in behaviour led to the formation of a special camp police force under Major Guy Lowther, which tracked down the perpetrators of this antisocial behaviour. The 'Exchange and Mart' shop also had to be on its guard when it was discovered that bags of sugar handed in for exchange were filled with salt and bars of chocolate were made of wood.

November slid into an arctic December. The Russians were still building up for the big offensive, while the Anglo-American forces were trying to hang up their washing on the Siegfried Line. In Oflag 79 one fact had to be faced – Christmas dinner would once again have to come from a Red Cross parcel.

12

The third and last Christmas

The cry of 'Home by Christmas' having subsided, most people turned their attention to saving up for the dinner – or, as it was termed, the 'Christmas bash'.

Saving was no easy matter on half a parcel. The problem of serving up also presented difficulties. During the first few months at Brunswick we had made good use of the electric power plugs in the walls. A wire contraption known as a brewer, dipped in a bowl of water and connected to the power plug, would brew our tea or coffee in a few minutes. The Germans were always on the look out for these brewers. Whenever a German appeared in a passage, there would be loud shouts of 'Goon up', and the brewer would be hidden before detection. The commandant became very annoyed by these brewers, and shortly before Christmas he threatened to cut off the electric current if any more were found in action. In order that the activities of the Canary should not be disturbed, the SBO instructed that all brewing machines should cease operations.

This did not affect us much, as we had our own stove and, provided that we could get enough fuel, the Christmas dinner would present no difficulties. The commandant then carried on a campaign against private stoves and the situation looked serious. A German officer came to inspect our stove, and much to our relief allowed it to remain.

Johnny, Paul and the old 'kriegies' of our party had a few reserve parcels up their sleeve. It was decided that these should be thrown into the Christmas bash. It was my job to think out a menu for the great day. We decided to have our big meal at lunchtime, and to spend the evening drinking a barrel of raisin wine that we had laid down several weeks before.

The great day arrived. All roll calls were cancelled, enabling us to have breakfast at a reasonable hour. We started our day with a large breakfast of porridge, scrambled eggs, bread, butter and marmalade. Although we appreciated this increase in our breakfast ration – the usual was two slices of bread and jam – it proved an unwise policy. We did not realize that our capacity for eating had diminished.

We lunched at one thirty. The menu comprised a hot mousse of tinned salmon on fried biscuit with a cheese sauce, fried meat roll with mashed potatoes and fried onions, and last but not least, the Christmas pudding. We had mixed the pudding a few days earlier; it consisted of crumbled bread, flour, prunes, raisins, jam, sugar, butter and a touch of raisin wine. The result was good – and heavy.

We started the meal confidently. The salmon went down well; the meat course, washed down with dark beer, provided no difficulties; we advanced on the pudding full of confidence. Dick Black and Mark Grant finished the meal without much effort, as did Delme Seymour Evans, but the rest of us were in difficulty halfway through the pudding. The two Archies and I plodded on. Paul announced that, given time, he would finished the course, but Johnny was in obvious trouble. He was, however, determined not to be defeated and stuck to his task with great courage. 'Slim' Somervel, a giant from the north country who had taken on the job of chef at the Rum Pot, came into the room during the final stages of Johnny's battle with the pudding and started to lay the odds against a finish.

Johnny won the day by literally pushing the last mouthful down his throat with a fork. He then collapsed on his bed. I drank a cup of coffee and then realized that I had overdone it. I felt as if I had a block of cement in my stomach. Breakfast had certainly been a mistake. Christmas dinner was a warning to us to take it easy when we got home.

Johnny and I had sufficiently recovered by the evening to eat a light supper and start on the raisin wine. We had made enough to have three litres each, most of which we were going to drink in the Rum Pot, where a gala had been arranged. The place was packed, and Tommy Sampson's band was in great form. The commandant had granted an extension until 1 a.m. The raisin wine had its effect and a good time was had by all.

The day ended on a cheerful note, and it was generally agreed that this really would be the last Christmas in captivity. The hangover on Boxing Day was painful, but it had been worth it.

The Rum Pot was granted another extension on New Year's Eve, when an even bigger crowd assembled. The management staged some good cabaret turns to entertain us between ten and midnight. At 11.30 p.m. Father Time, in the person of Alistair Bannerman, a member of the London stage, took the floor and reviewed from a scroll the various entertainments the theatre had provided over the past year.

On the stroke of midnight Tommy Sampson's band struck up in full blast. The lights went on and three 'glamour girls' dressed in white appeared on the floor. They threw cards to the audience that entitled the recipients to a 'free ticket to London in 1945'. 'Auld Lang Syne' was then sung in traditional style, and we left the Rum Pot in good spirits. A midnight service was being held further down the passage, the choir trying valiantly to outsing the blast of Tommy Sampson's trumpet, which reverberated through the cellars.

On 15 January, we heard the first news of the Russian offensive. The final phase had begun. Orders of the day from Moscow were good cocktails before the evening meal. Extra news flashes from the Canary came in throughout the day. The map experts were kept busy following up the breathtaking speed of the Russian advance.

The Germans, who for a long time had realized that we were getting the BBC news, made another attempt to locate the Canary. In the second week of January the Gestapo arrived in the camp, and the two buildings that housed the Canary were surrounded and searched. Once again, the wily bird escaped detection.

The further the Russians advanced, the more entangled the Germans became with their propaganda. The Bolshevik bogey had been painted in such startling colours for two years that it was only natural for every Russian advance to set a new flood of refugees in motion from the east. The High Command could hardly expect these people to stay put, when for two years they had been told that the Russians would murder and rape them on arrival. The more the situation deteriorated, the less was heard from the Nazi bosses. Hitler had completely withdrawn into the background. We were told that he spent his time building paper models for the reconstruction of Berlin. Statements were issued at intervals by people of little importance in the Party.

Our Prussian commandant disappeared one morning in mid-January and was later replaced by a more harmless individual. When the Russians reached the outskirts of Breslau the sub-commandant, an enormously fat creature, burst into tears. His wife and family lived in Breslau.

We had expected the end of the war so many times during the

past nine months that even the phenomenal advance from the east made us cautious in our forecast of the end. We were patiently watching for signs from the west that Montgomery was about to launch a final full-scale attack. By 2 February the Russians were only 165 miles from Brunswick – thirty miles nearer to us than the British forces.

The evening news bulletins were the only things that mattered. In this pent-up atmosphere some of the statements that came over the BBC were not without humour. At the time of the German withdrawal from their salient in the west, a leading London newspaper was quoted as saying: 'The Germans have three alternatives. To advance, to withdraw or to stay where they are.' Crystal clear, but not brilliant. On another occasion a well-known military spokesman was quoted: 'There is no doubt that the Russian aim is to destroy the German Army.' How did he guess?

13

Turnip time

By 16 February the camp supply of Red Cross parcels was exhausted. We were faced with the prospect of existing on German rations. The chaos caused by the Russian advance and the constant bombing of communications by the American and British Air Forces left us very little hope that further parcels would arrive. Unfortunately for us, the expiry of Red Cross supplies coincided with a cut in the German rations, on which we were now entirely dependent.

The greater part of our menu now consisted of turnips. This homely vegetable appeared on our table nearly every day, the cookhouse having succeeded in making it as unattractive as possible. The smell of turnips permeated all the rooms and passages. As room chef I was hard put to turn out either a filling or an attractive meal. Potato cakes, potatoes fried with turnips, potato soups, potato and bread puddings. What more can a man do with a potato and a turnip? Hunger set in, the weather remained cold, the heating was turned off except between the hours of 4 p.m. and 8 p.m., and the ration of cigarettes and tobacco sank lower and lower. It became increasingly difficult to obtain wood for our private cooking stoves. Tables, benches and doors disappeared in the night and the hundreds of little stoves burnt away merrily.

Conditions of hunger and discomfort bring out the worst and the best in a large community; in Oflag 79 the worst certainly predominated. The cigarette store was broken into and large quantities of cigarettes and tobacco were stolen. Meat disappeared from the cookhouse, bread from cupboards, and even the turnips must have felt in danger. Certain officers who, given the chance, would no doubt have eaten each other, stood in queues outside the cookhouse to collect surplus swill and spent the rest of the day washing the 'husks that the swine did eat'. The lack of food seemed to have washed away any sense of morality or self-respect this class of officer might once have possessed.

When rats infested the rubbish bins, rat poison in the form of biscuits was spread round these receptacles. A notice, no doubt for the benefit of the swill swallowers, was sent round the camp warning officers that these bits of biscuit were deadly poisonous.

A ridiculous inflation in cigarette prices was the next evil to raise its ugly head. Fifty cigarettes were sold for fifty pounds. Three small slabs of chocolate were sold for fifteen pounds! Everything was done by those in authority to stamp out this racket, but in a camp of two thousand men private transactions were impossible to suppress.

During this time the news was getting better and better, but hunger was sending our morale lower and lower. There was an air raid warning every evening, which meant sitting in total darkness between 8 and 10 p.m. The camp was on the direct route of the RAF 'Berlin Express' – a bombing line that operated every night from 22 February to 31 March.

Everything seemed to be conspiring to make our lives more uncomfortable. The heating was turned off, the water supply was hopelessly erratic, the weather was cold and the fuel for our private cooking became scarcer every day. We were given a certain amount of tea which we used to brew up just before going to bed. I remember one evening when our wood supply was very low, Johnny announced in a depressed voice: 'Well boys, if you want a hot drink tonight I'll have to burn my clogs, which I've had for three years!' The clogs were broken up and we had our tea. What sacrifices were made in prison life!

We certainly presented a picture of misery when we took our daily exercise on the concrete. Everyone was shedding weight, some more than others, but on average we all lost about a stone and a half after a month on German rations.

The days passed incredibly slowly, as we all felt so weak that the only thing to do was to spend most of the day in bed waiting for the next meal.

Telegraphic communications to and from Geneva were hopelessly erratic. Several telegrams were despatched to the Red Cross informing them of our plight and politely asking for assistance. At the beginning of March news was received that a truck had left Karlsruhe with fifteen hundred parcels addressed to our camp. Our numbers had by this time reached two and a half thousand, with the arrival of some American officers who had been made to walk most of the way from the Front. Thus the consignment, though a great help, was in the nature of a spit in the ocean.

During this difficult period a representative from the German

Foreign Office was attached to the camp. I never quite discovered what his duties were, but he appeared to be there to help the liaison between the British and the German commandant, and to make himself useful in any way possible. There is no doubt that he did his best to get hold of Red Cross supplies, and he seemed as anxious as anyone to get us enough to eat. The same thing applied to the new commandant, who proved himself a definite improvement on his predecessor.

On 18 March the eagerly awaited Karlsruhe truck arrived at the station practically intact, although it had been divebombed, machine-gunned and some of its contents pilfered *en route*. The contents of the parcels were spread out over the next three weeks, adding a good stiffening to the miserable German rations. Even this small addition to our larder sent morale sky high, and this reached greater heights on 24 March when, accompanied by brilliant spring weather, the Canary brought us news of numerous crossings over the Rhine. The Russians were also showing signs of mammoth activity in the east. We were nicely sandwiched between the two advancing fronts, being roughly a hundred and fifty miles from each.

We got news of other soldiers' camps in Germany when a British medical officer, who had been attached to several working camps, arrived in our midst. He reported that the German guards were becoming positively servile to the British soldiers working in the various areas. The black market was extensive, and in many cases German guards were asking their prisoners for good conduct slips to show to the British or American troops on arrival! Many of these slips were sold for tobacco or schnapps; in several cases where the recipient did not understand English, the good conduct slip actually announced, 'This man is a bastard; cut his throat.'

The most tantalizing piece of news that the medical officer reported was the existence at Lübeck (120 miles distant) of dumps containing a million Red Cross parcels. The Germans had neither petrol nor rolling stock to circulate this enormous supply, and Red Cross lorries were also said to be stranded at Lübeck through lack of fuel. At the same time, Geneva announced over the wireless that Red Cross road convoys had left Switzerland by road in order to supply the various camps with food. From then on, every lorry that appeared on the nearby autobahn was closely inspected for the welcome sign of the Red Cross!

The news of the great breakthrough on the Rhine reached us on

27 March. I always feel that it was the gardening that did the trick. A week before that momentous happening we had been issued with gardening tools. Each room was given a strip of ground in which to plant vegetables. Whenever anyone dug a garden in a prison camp, something happened – usually a move of some sort. Tom Bond took over our strip. He worked like a slave to make sure something would happen. 'If onions won't do the trick, I'll plant a vegetable marrow,' said Tom.

No sooner were the onions in the ground than General Eisenhower and Field Marshal Montgomery started off. Within three days, the German armies in the west were routed and we were left with our onions to await the arrival of our troops, still gloomily watched over by our seventy-year-old guards.

Morale went sky high, even on empty stomachs. A young officer caught stealing potatoes was flogged by his fellow subalterns and then thrown into a bomb crater filled with sewage water. Things were looking up!

On the morning of 29 March a truck from Lübeck arrived in the camp. The news flashed round that parcels had arrived at last. Reserves were thrown into the frying pan to celebrate the event. During breakfast a further message was received. The truck was from Lübeck, but it was a YMCA vehicle and not a Red Cross one. It had delivered skates, ice hockey sticks and toilet paper!

By 30 March the breakthrough from the Rhine was complete. It could now only be a matter of days. The end of turnip time was in sight.

14
Finale

April 1945 turned out to be a month crammed full of incidents – a month of hope, anxiety, disappointment, impatience, relief and liberation. I do not expect ever again to pass through a period in which each event is etched so sharply in my memory.

We started the month badly. The food ration seemed to grow smaller and smaller. It was difficult to appreciate the splendid news from the Front – malnutrition was taking the gilt off the gingerbread. It was interesting to note during this period of acute hunger how strong the craving for nicotine can be among those who regard cigarette smoking as the greatest of all human needs. Two colonels and a padré were admitted to hospital suffering from malnutrition simply because they had exchanged what little food they had for cigarettes.

On 5 April a lorry arrived from Lübeck with one thousand American parcels, which did much to raise morale. It is incredible what a difference a few extra mouthfuls of food can make when one is really hungry.

Looking back on those last ten days of captivity, I think that next to hunger, rumour was our worst enemy. As the Americans advanced so the rumours increased, many of them started by the German guards. The rumours always grossly exaggerated the American advance, so when the true distances were announced by the BBC – and Heaven knows they were good enough – we became disappointed and impatient.

The German officers and guards were quite prepared for the end – in fact I think they were nearly as anxious as we were to see the finish. There was no question of their putting up any resistance when the Americans arrived, and during the last few days the sentries used to go to their platforms with suitcases ready packed so that when they themselves were marched off to captivity they would have all their belongings with them.

On 8 April the American Army was only nineteen miles from Brunswick. The following night we watched huge fires burning over Hanover, and on the evening of 10 April gunfire was heard a few miles south of Brunswick. Fighter bombers appeared in the sky and we spent the early part of the evening watching the planes applying the 'softening up' process to various positions in and around the town. That night was one of the noisiest I have experienced. The Americans were shelling Brunswick, and the Germans were carrying out demolitions on the nearby aerodrome. It was impossible for us to tell what was happening. We sat up all night smoking our few remaining cigarettes. The general opinion was that the Americans would put in a dawn attack to capture the town. We were wrong again. The next day, 11 April, passed very quietly. Life went on as usual, and with the exception of a few fighter bombers little was seen or heard to indicate the approach of the Americans. In fact the armoured spearheads had bypassed Brunswick and were well on their way to Magdeburg. The day dragged on, and we prepared for another noisy night. But the Germans had finished their demolition and the Americans did not shell Brunswick. We all slept well and awoke refreshed to welcome the greatest day of our lives.

We were just starting on our breakfast of ersatz coffee and brown bread when the moment arrived. I looked at Archie Noel's watch – the only one in the room that was working; the time was 9.35 a.m. We heard wild shouts in the passage. 'The boys are here.'

I had often wondered what it would be like, and how we would feel. Now that the end had come we could hardly believe it. We remained very calm and quiet, congratulated each other, and then went on with our breakfast. I think we all felt like weeping – that was probably why we showed little outward sign of excitement.

The 'Old Master', Tom Bond, was an exception. He was lying in his top bunk bed when he heard the shouts. A wild look came into his eyes. With a shout like an Indian war chief he leapt from his bunk and rushed from the room, his pyjama trousers slipping down his legs. The two Archies, who had both completed nearly five years of captivity, showed remarkable restraint.

It was a great moment. The curtain was at last being brought down on this unpleasant drama. We were free to venture forth into the outside world.

Our liberator was an American sergeant of C. Troop 125th Cavalry Squadron, 30th Infantry Division of the Ninth Army, who had driven up to the gates in a jeep. The German soldier on the gate had signalled him in as if he was an important visitor who had long been expected. He was followed shortly afterwards by Captain

Ploehn with other soldiers of the 125th Cavalry Squadron. The German guard company were disarmed and marched out of the gates by the American sergeant, rifle cocked under his arm. One of the Germans, who was late in falling in, received a sharp reminder in the seat of his pants.

During the day staff cars, jeeps, anti-tank guns and war correspondents poured into the camp. We were told to stay inside the wire. Most of us were so dazed that we had no desire to go out. Several British officers arrived during the afternoon. It was a strange coincidence that one of the first to appear was Captain Bill Greenwood, who had been with us at Fontanellato. He had escaped to Switzerland after the Italian Armistice.

A thanksgiving service was held inside the wire during the afternoon. We sang 'Praise My Soul The King Of Heaven', and other hymns suitable to the great occasion.

It was only natural that after the first shock of liberation our thoughts should turn once more to food. Within a few hours of the arrival of the Americans we started an orgy of eating and drinking. The lid was blown off the German 'no food' story. Hundreds of stale loaves of bread (which should have been given to us) were found in the German store house, together with tons of potatoes, boxes of margarine, sausage pâté and a hundred thousand tins of pork. In the meantime every type of wine was arriving from Brunswick. It was not unnatural that we sat down to eat and drink unwisely. We gave our contracted stomachs little chance – I will draw a veil over the consequences.

In Brunswick and the surrounding district a chaotic state of affairs prevailed. Hundreds of foreign workers, mostly Russians, Poles and French, had been housed in and around Brunswick for the past two years. They too had been waiting for this moment, and when they were let loose they set out to enjoy themselves. The French took matters quite calmly and many of them set off to walk back to France. The Russians and Poles had other plans. Any surviving shops in Brunswick were smashed and looted. The wine cellars were broken into and hock, gin and rum were consumed in enormous quantities by the liberated workers. Much good wine was wasted, as the looters did not stop to draw the corks. The necks of the bottles were smashed and the liquor poured down their throats and over their faces. A drunk Russian who had been a slave worker for two years naturally took an even more moderate view of the Germans than he did when sober! Shooting followed on the heels of looting. The Russians were taking it out on any German they could lay their hands on. The American soldiers, who were very thin on the ground, had the difficult job of keeping order, but they tackled it as best they could.

At the aerodrome next door to the camp the sumptuous Luftwaffe quarters were looted from top to bottom. The magnificent kitchens and officers' mess were completely wrecked. Anything edible or drinkable was immediately consumed by the hungry workers. Two days after liberation we were allowed outside the wire. The first place I visited was the Luftwaffe quarters. Though badly smashed up, it was plain to see the luxury in which Goering's men had lived. The men's married quarters were as luxurious as any West End flat. In the buildings around the hangars, thousands of pounds' worth of equipment and machine tools were scattered over the floors. It was an amazing sight.

German-speaking officers were allowed into Brunswick to help the Americans. They were quickly followed by a crowd of others, who invented every conceivable excuse to get into the town and live in comparative comfort at the one decent hotel. I went into Brunswick myself and was struck by the fact that most of our interpreters and their helpers had given themselves the job of looking after the various wine cellars in the town. I also felt it my duty to investigate the wine situation, and with the help of a charming American soldier I returned to camp on a lorry carrying fifty bottles of gin and a splendid assortment of hocks.

Once the wine situation was under control the motor car industry was looked into, and within three days every form of civilian car appeared in the camp. Petrol left on the airfield by the Germans solved the fuel problem. Mercedes and Opels appeared to be the most popular makes; our room was not as quick off the mark as usual, and we had to be content with the commandant's two-horse buggy, which was admirably handled by 'coachman' Dick Black. Dick toured round the countryside visiting farms where he procured eggs, chickens, fresh white bread, milk and other delicacies. He was always accompanied by one or two passengers who carried rifles, just in case there should be any arguments. After a few days he became known as the local Dick Turpin, and the bloated German farmers produced their goods without any argument or payment.

I walked round a few of the nearby villages. The local inhabitants were so terrified of the Russians that they were quite pleased to see

British or Americans. They grossly exaggerated the stories of the Russians. Tom and I were walking round one village with two American soldiers when three very scared women implored our help as there were 'a hundred Russians looting and raping in the village'. On investigation, we discovered one rather bored Russian worker sitting in the local public house. It was very satisfactory to see the Germans in a terrified and cowed condition. They realized the sins that they and their countrymen had been committing for the last ten years, but they did not relish being given a dose of their own medicine.

No praise can be too high for the manner in which the American soldiers dealt with the Germans. There was no question of fraternizing and no false sentiment. They had a job to do and they were determined to see that the Germans got what they deserved. I am convinced that wherever the American Army of Occupation was in control, the Germans got the treatment they deserved. There was absolutely no cruelty in their methods – just absolute firmness and a determination to teach the Germans the lessons they should have been taught twenty-five years ago.

I suppose a prisoner of war is never satisfied and always impatient. After a few days of freedom we began to get restless. When were we going to be taken home? How were we going to be taken home? The usual rumours and hopes sprang up, followed by the usual disappointments. First we were told that we would go to Brussels by truck; then it was stated that we would go by air. I don't think anyone minded how we went, so long as we got away from Germany and its gloomy ruins. Brunswick was like a city of the dead – streets and streets of shattered buildings.

On 16 April a convoy of trucks arrived in the camp and took away the first two hundred of us. The rest of the inmates were to be flown home the next day. We packed our bags and stood by – a most exciting moment for all of us. The planes were coming to our aerodrome, so all we had to do was to walk through the pine wood and board the planes. At the last moment the planes were required for more urgent work, and this started a series of disappointments. Every day for the next five days the planes were coming, but there was always a hitch and the move was put off to the morrow. Looking back on it, one realizes how ridiculous our impatience was, but if you have been waiting for something for years, a day's delay at the very end seems like a month. Each time the move was postponed we vowed we would get hold of a car and make our own way back. On 21 April a couple of German tanks were reported to be roaming the countryside. The Americans set off to liquidate them. This provided an excuse to go away on our own. Supposing a German tank got into the camp for just half an hour! There was no defence and only a handful of Americans. That was the argument we used among ourselves simply because we needed some impetus to get us on our way. We didn't really believe the tank story!

On the Sunday morning of 22 April, ten days after our liberation, Van Burton came to Dick and me and told us that he had arranged for three seats in a Mercedes Benz that was leaving for Brussels in half an hour. That settled it. Dick and I collected the few belongings we wished to take home, bid goodbye to the rest of the room, and together with Van went off to join the car, which was waiting just outside the wire.

The car, which belonged to a prosperous Brunswick citizen, had been politely requisitioned by Roy Cook, an officer who had been closely connected with the theatrical activities in the camp. The fifth member of the party was John Firth, one of the leading artists of Oflag 79. The Mercedes, painted black with a chromium line, was most impressive and very comfortable.

The feeling of relief as we drove away from the camp – never to see that infernal wire fence again – was overwhelming. We passed through Hanover shortly before lunchtime. We had heard, and had seen from a distance many a time, that the city had been badly smashed by the Anglo-American bombing, but even so we were astonished at the scene of utter destruction. It is impossible to describe the spectacle of these bombed-out cities. Street after street of rubble, with hardly a living soul to be seen.

After passing through Hanover we stopped at a prosperous-looking farmhouse and ordered the inhabitants to give us lunch. There was no argument. We ate our lunch and drove off.

The autobahns were in perfect condition. The Germans had blown all the bridges, but the Americans had erected new ones with amazing rapidity. As we drove west we passed a constant stream of motor convoys taking ammunition and supplies to the Front, and little parties of French foreign workers trudging back to France, pushing their belongings in old prams with the tricolour bravely flapping on top of the baggage. Whenever we wanted more petrol we drew up alongside the first American truck we saw and they gave us all we required. The kindness and generosity of the Americans from the time we were liberated until we reached

England was beyond all description. Nothing was too much trouble for them; they went out of their way to do everything to help us.

We reached Münster at about 6 p.m. All the towns we had passed through showed the havoc caused by our air raids, but the country in between showed little signs of warfare. Presumably the American advance had been one dash from town to town. At Münster we were royally entertained by the AMGOT authorities. An early start had been arranged for the following morning, but the celebrations of the night before prevented us from making any sense before eleven o'clock, and even then we were in a very delicate condition.

We crossed the Rhine at Wesel, or rather what had once been Wesel. The mass of ruins gave us our first glimpse of what modern warfare can do to a town. It was a devastating sight.

At 1.55 p.m. (I carefully noted the time, as I considered it a great moment in my life) we crossed the German frontier into Holland. Pray God I never have to go back to Germany. Everything seemed more cheerful as soon as we had left the dreary 'Goons'. We had left behind a civilian population living in terror of the foreign workers whom they themselves had treated as slaves for the past four years. We left them to reap the fruits of their aggression.

We arrived in Brussels shortly before 8 p.m. and drove to the town major's office. The city was looking its best, the lilac and may trees in full bloom. We were directed to the hostels specially organized for returning POWs and run by the Belgian branch of the WVS.

We felt that we had stolen a march on the friends we had left at Oflag 79. This was, however, not the case. We reached the door of the hostel at exactly the same moment as several truckloads of officers from 79. They had just driven in from Brussels airport, having flown from Brunswick that afternoon. They told us that hundeds of Dakotas had landed on the airfield, whereupon the highly organized evacuation scheme had turned into a free for all rush to the nearest plane. As the last officers had left the wire the foreign workers were lined up outside, waiting to go in and continue the joys of looting. They were certainly welcome to the belongings I had left behind! One of the Dakota pilots had also decided to have a look round the area in search of a motorcycle to take back with him. He was gone for about an hour before returning with his plunder. Meanwhile, his passengers were champing with impatience. 'I am so sorry. I hope you haven't been waiting long,' said the pilot. 'Only three and a half years', replied an old and worn out 'kriegie'.

The organization of the Brussels hostels was first class. The Belgian WVS girls were charming, and they worked untiringly to make us comfortable.

We spent two nights in Brussels. The city seemed very gay, but the prices were fantastic. I dined with officers of the Brussels garrison. Their mess consisted of the entire first floor of the Palace Hotel, including restaurant, cocktail bar and sitting rooms. Soldiering at its best!

On Wednesday 25 April we drove out to the airport. Our party consisted of about four hundred officers. When we arrived on the field a long line of forty-seater Dakotas was waiting to take us on the last lap of our journey home. Our plane was very full, and I had to sit on the floor. But what matter, when you are on your way home? The American pilot climbed into the plane and asked us in a most charming manner, 'Are you guys ready to go home?' In a few minutes the engines were roaring and we climbed up into a bright blue sky.

I had a somewhat unromantic flight home, as within five minutes of taking off the officer at whose feet I was sitting began to be sick into the bucket the Americans had thoughtfully supplied. The unfortunate man continued to be ill throughout the flight, and soon after we crossed the Channel I followed suit, more out of sympathy than anything else.

We landed at a large and (to us) new aerodrome between Aylesbury and Oxford. As the plane circled round before landing we could see the flag-bedecked hangar and the words WELCOME HOME written in large red letters on a white background.

It was a thrilling moment, stepping out of the plane and standing in the long grass breathing in the first smell of the English countryside. Everything looked so lovely. No one could have wished for a more perfect afternoon. One has only to go away from England for a year or two to realize that there is something about the English countryside that looks, smells and feels different from anywhere else. How lucky we were to be coming back in spring, with everything clean and unspoiled to welcome us.

There are many things I shall remember and many things I shall forget about the war, captivity and release. But I shall never forget that golden moment when I stepped out of the plane and stood in the long grass, drinking in the joys of an English spring day.

We were shepherded off to a large hangar gaily decorated with flags. Half the floor space was partitioned off for the medical examination and on the other half were long tables on which was set a splendid tea. Everything was most efficiently run. Instructions were called out through a loudspeaker, and before we knew where we were we were facing yet another delousing spray!

WAAFs and civilian helpers then conducted us to the tables and gave us tea. The kindness of everyone was quite overwhelming. It may sound stupid, but I felt a lump in my throat and tears in my eyes. I had never dreamed that from the very start we should have such a wonderful welcome home.

After tea we got into army lorries and were driven several miles to a reception camp near Taplow. As we passed through the towns and villages people cheered and waved. We might have been conquering heroes returning home instead of a bunch of broken down gaolbirds. It was all the more wonderful because it was all so utterly unexpected. We were so overcome by it all that we remained speechless.

We stayed that night at the reception camp, where everything possible was done for us. It gave us twenty-four hours to get over the emotional strain of the homecoming and time to brace ourselves up for the biggest thrill of all – meeting our families. Family reunions are purely personal, and can be of no interest in this book. I will just say that mine was as wonderful as I had always hoped it would be.

So the story is ended. The war in Europe is ended, and the future is as uncertain as it has ever been. There are many changes and many faces we will never see again. If a great part of our war effort had been spent sitting behind a wire fence, we can at least now join the ranks of the millions of men and women who are determined that this tragedy will never be repeated.